# COWBOY
## *Chic*
### WESTERN STYLE COMES HOME

# COWBOY Chic

## WESTERN STYLE COMES HOME

CHASE
REYNOLDS
EWALD

GIBBS·SMITH
P
PUBLISHER

SALT LAKE CITY

# For Charles

First Edition
05 04 03 02 01      5 4 3 2

Published by
Gibbs Smith, Publisher
P.O. Box 667
Layton, Utah 84041

Orders: (1-800) 748-5439
Web site: www.gibbs-smith.com

Designed and produced by J. Scott Knudsen,
Park City, Utah
Printed and bound in Korea

**Library of Congress Cataloging-in-Publication Data**

Ewald, Chase Reynolds, 1963–
    Cowboy Chic
    Chase Reynolds Ewald.—1st ed.
      p. cm.
    ISBN 0-87905-962-1
    1. Interior decoration—West (U.S.)  I. Title.
NK2008 .E96 2000
747.218—dc21
                          00-029722

# CONTENTS

# Acknowledgements

Every project like this takes on a life of its own. There are so many involved—from those who contribute to it to those who, through no choice of their own, have to put up with it—that mere thanks don't seem adequate. That said, I most certainly would like to thank a number of people, including Sue and John Gallagher and Al and Ann Simpson for their gracious hospitality on numerous occasions. A fine eye defines the work of photographers Dewey Vanderhoff, Elijah Cobb, David Swift, and Lynn Donaldson, and of designers Brian Goff of Harker Design, architect Kirk Michels, Van Bryan of Apogee Architects, Debbie Hindman of Associates III, and Robin Stater of Sierra Design Studio. Marty Kruzich of Martin-Harris Gallery in Jackson and Bob Brown of the Big Horn Gallery in Cody should both be commended for their unflagging support of furniture as fine art over the past decade.

For sharing their collections, I am particularly grateful to Eric and Stacey Ossorio, Don and Vicky Smith, Bo and Anna Polk, Mary Lou and Willis McDonald, and Edgar and Margery Massinter. Lee Molesworth, Sarah Thorne, and Wally Reber gave graciously of their time, opinions, and memories. We all owe an enormous debt to Mike Patrick, Thea Marx, and the entire Board of Trustees of the Western Design Conference, who have created a spectacular showcase for contemporary western design, and to all the craftspeople whose artistry, enthusiasm, and willingness to share brings western design firmly into the twenty-first century.

I appreciate enormously Kerry Strike, who was unfailingly upbeat in her pursuit of historic photographs; my agent, Diana Finch, for making time when it matters; and Madge Baird, who for three books in a row has been remarkably organized and professional, and who took it all in stride when the delivery of a baby interrupted the delivery of a manuscript.

*Obrigada, merci,* and thanks to Marivone, Flor, Nanon, and my mom, able field marshals during the campaign. I owe a lot to Addie, Jessie, and Ross, who demonstrate every day that furniture has to withstand abuse as well as look pretty, and to Katherine, who rode along with me every step of the way. And most of all, my love and thanks to Charles, who taught me that you can't know about a piece of furniture until you've crawled underneath it.

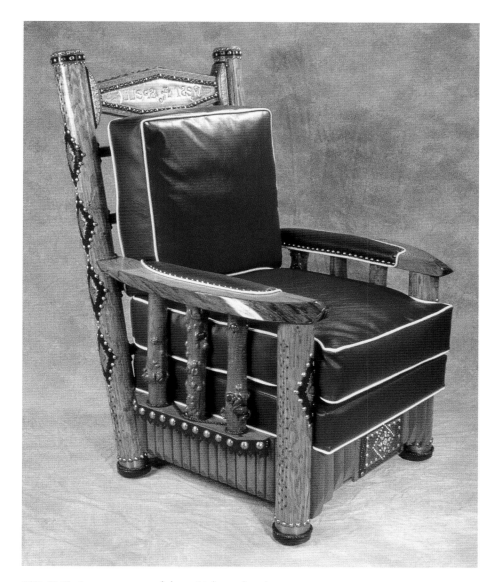

*T.B. McCoy's interpretation of classic Molesworth style* Photo courtesy of the artist.

# Introduction

When I was eighteen and about to start college in the East, I went west. I was headed for a wrangling job in Wyoming, having been captivated by the grandeur of the western landscape ever since I'd spent three summers at a camp in Jackson Hole as a young girl. My destination was a historic dude ranch an hour from the nearest town, tucked at the end of a dead-end valley surrounded by wilderness.

Although my preconceptions were vivid, they paled in comparison to reality. The Upper South Fork Valley, forty-five miles south of Cody, was grand and dramatic and awesomely beautiful. Foothills rising to vertical cliffs that formed the valley walls; cottonwoods along the river and aspen groves along the creeks; moose and deer hiding among the willows; coyotes loping across the hayfields at sunset; antelope, elk, and bighorn sheep on the high sagebrush flats; eagles and red-tailed hawks gliding overhead; and the river running through it all—this was the stuff of fantasy.

The lifestyle captured my imagination as well. I thought it a privilege to rise at five and ride in the dark up into the foothills, gather the ranch horses from a 2,000-acre "pasture," ford a sometimes raging river, and run the herd down a cottonwood-shaded dirt lane from the river. We burst into the open space next to the old trading post and galloped past the camera-clicking guests into the corral in time for breakfast. Never mind that after the second day of seven hours riding I was almost paralyzed. After a few weeks of this schedule, I was literally falling asleep in the saddle.

The ranch ambience was as evocative as the old log buildings used as the set for *Shane* that we used to ride to back in my camp days. Only this was no ghost town; these buildings had been used for eighty years: the trading post, with its Navajo rugs and old glass-fronted cubbyholes from the days the ranch served as the area's post office; the wrangler's tack shed, with its ancient pot-bellied stove still stoked every morning and a wooden countertop, well-worn with grooves and chips from decades of repairing broken latigos; the wranglers' barn, with its concave dirt floor, hollowed out from years of booted wranglers leading shod horses in for their feed; and the springhouse, with its wild array of growth atop its sod roof, stainless-steel ladles hanging on its wall to dip cold, pure water from the spring that flowed from underneath it. The old blacksmith shop, tools arrayed on the

*The myth of the West—a collective national representation of American character as forged by the frontier and embodied by the cowboy, set against a background of dramatic beauty—lives today in scenery that is both awesome and timeless.* Photo © 2000 Chase Reynolds Ewald.

walls, was still a great place to shoe horses, even if no one fired up the traditional forge anymore.

The privy nearest to the corral was decorated with an elaborate mural painted by the owner's daughter; festooned overhead like party streamers hung sleeping bats that never seemed to mind the squeaking of the opening door. The "Gossip Tree," a bench-encircled cottonwood, was a welcoming place to visit before meals. And there was "Amen Corner" in an old soddy next to the phone room. The rest of the ranch was just as evocative: the dining room with its long tables, yellow Fiesta-ware pitchers, and wood-burning stove; the staff cabins of rough-hewn planks, spartan in their simplicity; the lodge living room with its mounted heads, built-in seating, fireplace screen with the ranch brand, antler candelabras, and table lamps with painted shades bearing cowboy-and-Indian motifs designed by legendary local furniture maker Thomas Molesworth.

Molesworth furniture—such as the red-leather-and-burl armchairs in the living room and a hundred custom-made beds scattered throughout the guest cabins—set the tone for the interiors, along with Old Hickory chairs, many of which had been re-covered in rawhide when their rush seats had given out. There were also fifty-year-old rustic pieces by unknown ranch hands—such as the chairs made from old nail barrels, and the milk cans with tractor seats nailed on that might have been made by a fellow everyone knew only as Jonesie. Cabins were furnished simply for staff: iron-frame single beds, chests of drawers and mirrors, sturdy wooden

*An atmosphere redolent of cowboys-and-Indians culture brought dudes back to the best guest ranches time and again, generation after generation. The trading post at the Valley Ranch in Cody, Wyoming, was filled in its heyday with Native American artifacts now owned by the Buffalo Bill Historical Center.*
Photo courtesy Sarah Thorne Mentock.

chairs snugged up under compact wooden desks for writing letters home, and a woodstove. Guest cabins ranged from the ascetic to the "Little Waldorf," a three-room cabin with stone fireplaces and a full suite of Molesworth furniture and Navajo rugs.

The ranch activities were as timeless as the buildings: Percheron-drawn hayrides, weekly square dances on the warped floor of the old rec hall, and Saturday rodeos staged for each group of guests. Only a few details, like the daily wood delivery to each cabin by a small cart pulled by a miniature horse, occasionally reminded us that our lifestyle was in large part showmanship.

Although the ranch had enough cattle to necessitate our riding over to neighboring pastures once in a while to gather them back, and grew enough hay that we spent many August evenings bucking bales, its main business was dudes. They came from New York and Denver and Los Angeles, from Germany and Australia and other far-flung points. They stayed a week, dressed like cowboys, ate hearty ranch food, rode horses all day, fished as desired, and left pretension at home. Some came just once, to "do the West" with their kids, while others continued a family tradition that had started back in the twenties or thirties.

Then as now, they came for the grandeur of the scenery, a chance to experience the ranch lifestyle, an excuse not to dress for dinner. Both dudes and staff came to live out a fantasy firmly established in the American mind, first by railroad promoters, then by Hollywood, by television, by dime novels, by radio serializations, and, in more recent years, by country-western megaperformers and high-profile rodeo stars.

We were all drawn together by the myth of the West, a collective national representation of American character forged by the frontier, ennobled by the grand vistas, and embodied by the cowboy. It's a myth that still lives today, one that still attracts thousands to dude ranches and millions to the American West's national parks. Of late, however, that yearning has evolved. Certain regions of the Rocky Mountain West have experienced some of the most rapid growth in the country as advances in technology, communication, and travel have made it easier to do business in hard-to-reach places. As major urban centers—and along with them, urban problems—have expanded, the pace of families fleeing cities and overcrowded suburbs in search of a more meaningful, less stressful lifestyle has accelerated. The West as a place of retreat and renewal has never been more popular. Whether it's a home on a mountainside near trendy Aspen, a refurbished cabin on a creek in Wyoming, or a full-scale cattle ranch surrounded by jaw-dropping scenery in a celebrity-studded valley in Montana, the appeal of having one's own little slice of the West has never been stronger.

As this desire to have one's own refuge has evolved, so too have the furnishings for that refuge. Western style is no longer defined by wagon-wheel chandeliers, horse-collar mirrors, and horseshoe-and-lariat motifs. While these icons still exist and are being pressed into service in ways that are fun and whimsical without always being kitschy, western style has grown up. In addition to the seemingly ubiquitous Thomas Molesworth–inspired furniture of applied pole, routed scenes on inset panels, burled wood, and weavings from the New Mexico town of Chimayo, western furnishings today range from meticulous leather-wrapped armoires to petrified-stone table-tops on fantastically curved and striated juniper bases, from headboards inset with strips of Indian beadwork to rustic desks made from woods not traditionally western. While there are still plenty of mounted heads on walls in the West, lighting fixtures range from the traditional cut-metal sil-houettes to three-dimensional cast-bronze pieces by fine artists. The river-rock fireplace still pre-dominates, but there's also a place for the hand-carved mantelpiece depicting a trout stream or some local wildlife—representing hundreds of hours of painstaking work.

This extraordinary commitment of time plus a pure passion and singular creative vision are the hallmarks of the fine furnishings of the contem-porary West. Today's artisans—whether they're

*On dude ranches and working ranches alike, accommodations for staff were spartan, a fact that in no way lessened the romantic appeal of the western lifestyle. This typical bunkhouse was "decorated" with a utilitarian woodstove and various tools of the cowboy trade.* Photo courtesy Buffalo Bill Historical Center, Cody, Wyoming; Charles Belden Collection.

actually working in the Rocky Mountain West or, in some cases, simply making furniture that feels at home in the West—are creating works that are fresh, beautiful, meticulously crafted, sometimes nostalgic, often humorous, and always celebratory of both the region and its traditions.

The craftsmanship featured in the following pages evokes the West of the past while embrac-ing the future. Its contemporary interpretations convey as comfortable a familiarity as did the old "Gossip Tree" back at the ranch, where guests visited while waiting for the dinner bell to ring. Just as the changing West maintains an aura of timelessness due to its vastness and grandeur, today's cowboy chic represents an evolution in sophistication that is ever at home in the American West.

# Westward Ho!

## FUNCTION OVER FORM

A cartoon for contemporary western furniture makers might look something like this: In the first panel, a group of pioneers, their covered wagon in the background, are eating dinner around a campfire; they're seated on roughly cut stumps. In the second panel, several members of a homesteading family, pictured in front of their one-room soddy at a table of rough-hewn planks, perch on crude benches made from bark-covered half-logs. In the third, the family, prosperous now by dint of hard work and personal fortitude, sit stiffly posed in the living room of their frame house, which is furnished with Victorian carved-mahogany furniture, velvet drapes, and oriental carpets. In the fourth frame, the same settlers' grown-up grandchildren are pictured working at their computers from their cathedral-ceiling log home; there is fine art on the wall, a stunning view out the window, and a fabulous built-in desk and bookshelves with a matching chair. The casework has twigs all over it; the chair, of course, is fashioned from a stump.

The desire to connect with the past is perhaps stronger in the West than in any other region known for its rustic-furniture traditions. The West, after all, has long been the national repository for our dreams. The myth and romance of the West—with its long-lived images of noble Indians, rugged mountain men, daring explorers, stalwart cowboys, and courageous pioneer families following the golden globe westward—has shaped our identity, our very sense of who we are as Americans. For a century and a half, the unbounded vastness of the West has represented a place to reinvent oneself, a place to make a new start, and a place to escape—whether from the law or from religious intolerance or simply from bad luck. In recent decades it has become a refuge for those fleeing the pressures of an increasingly urbanized and industrialized world.

The history of western furniture is fairly short and simple: until the white man came along and built low, squat, hand-hewn log cabins for overwintering, the peoples were nomadic, saving their expressions of fine art for their beaded moccasins and painted tepees. The fur trappers (and traders, who were itinerant)—the first non-natives to venture into the interior West from the early to the mid-1800s—would have been semi-nomadic too as they trapped out one river system

*A true western style was slow to evolve. In the early part of the century, it might have mixed wicker chairs, cloth curtains, Navajo rugs, and pole furniture with a massive set of moose antlers over the fireplace.*
Photo courtesy Park County Historical Society Archives.

after another. When the weather got harsh, they would have relied on a crude log cabin and a few pieces of rough, functional furniture, probably fashioned from stumps and half-logs. Their axes wouldn't have allowed for much fine detail work, and they wouldn't have noticed.

As the West was opened up for settlement with the establishment in the 1840s of the Oregon Trail, among others, settlers started flowing westward; the flow escalated to a cascade after the Civil War ended in 1865. When gold was struck in California in 1848, and in the interior West from 1850–1870, hordes of young adventure-seekers, visions of fortune dancing in their heads, streamed west. Fleeing religious

persecution, thousands of Mormons headed for the Great Salt Lake in the 1840s and '50s. With the forging of the Texas cattle trails to the midwestern railheads in the 1860s and '70s, cowboys started trailing northward, many eventually staying to found cattle ranches. After these arrivals had built a roof over their heads, they would, of course, have needed somewhere to sit.

Early western furnishings were made from the materials on hand, which—before a steady

*Those settlers who prospered looked East for their furnishings in a desire to put their mark on the land and to convince themselves that they actually had carved a lasting home out of the wilderness. The grandeur of turn-of-the-century western hotels, such as the Irma, built by Buffalo Bill in his namesake town of Cody in 1902, were often furnished in the height of Victorian elegance.* Photo courtesy Buffalo Bill Historical Center, Cody, WY.

supply of goods was brought by the railroads—generally didn't include nails. The absence of nails meant that joinery had to be fairly sophisticated, mainly mortise-and-tenon and dovetail. But the tools and techniques were primitive, and the furniture that resulted wasn't so much a design statement as it was a style born of necessity. If it was comfortable, that was a bonus. Function was the top priority. Recycling and "making do," a mantra of the early West, would have been a natural consequence—hence the rise of cowhide-covered chairs and tables made from wagon wheels. Decoration would have been served by functional items such as blankets, baskets, and pottery. There wasn't time to be picky about knotholes or uneven timbers.

As life got slightly more comfortable in the territories, craftsmen began trying to duplicate images they had seen in other places. Those in the Southwest (which because of its long history already had a distinctive style) looked to Spain while those in the interior West looked to the East Coast and to Europe for their inspiration. These craftsmen were limited to the materials and tools on hand, however, and the resulting furniture was a folksy approximation of the original.

## TRUE WEST

A true western style was slow to develop over the course of the following decades. The settlement of the West has been glamorized by Hollywood and novelists, but the people who lived through it suffered great hardships, including isolation, disease, lack of supplies, and a vicious climate. Those who survived and prospered would have looked East for their furnishings in a desire to put their mark on the land and to convince themselves that they had carved a lasting home out of the wilderness. Not for them wagon-wheel tables, if they could help it; they were much more likely to order Gustav Stickley Mission-style oak furniture from Sears, Roebuck or Montgomery Ward or decorate in the Victorian style that had prevailed for some decades. With greater ease of travel and the establishment of numerous railroad lines throughout the region (the Pacific, the first transcontinental railroad, was completed in 1869), this became a possibility for more and more people.

Relative ease of travel drew the first real tourist-adventurers and hunters who were attracted to the region by unbelievable descriptions of towering mountains, clear-flowing rivers,

a picturesque native people, and, above all, vast quantities of game. These wonders were heavily promoted by the railroads, and no one capitalized on this drama more than Buffalo Bill Cody, who not only took his Wild West Show across the world but also brought wealthy sportsmen to the West. Cody's Pahaska Tepee Lodge, built next to Yellowstone Park in 1905, was an early example of western rustic style; similarly, the tone for national-park architecture was set in buildings like the 1904 Old Faithful Inn in Yellowstone.

*Hunting lodges, such as Buffalo Bill's Pahaska Tepee, constructed from 1903 to 1905 on the eastern edge of Yellowstone National Park, were built to reflect the rugged nature of the wilderness outside. Rough logs, cavernous fireplaces, simple sturdy furniture, and trophies of the hunt were typical furnishings.*
Photo courtesy Buffalo Bill Historical Center, Cody, WY.

*The advent of the railroads into the interior West made it feasible and affordable to import furniture, such as these rustic Old Hickory chairs from Indiana.* Photo courtesy National Park Service.

These structures and some of their furnishings drew on the rustic traditions firmly established in the Appalachian Mountains, along the Great Lakes, and, most notably, in the Adirondacks. There, immense log camp buildings designed by William West Durant and others as early as the 1870s were decked out with furniture made from twigs and roots by local woodsmen needing winter work and, later, craftsmen such as Ernest Stowe in the early 1900s. Cody's Pahaska Tepee lodge was designed by New York artist A. A.

Anderson, who had been inspired by rustic retreats of that region. The rustic architecture of the Old Faithful Inn was the product of precepts set forth by Frederick Law Olmsted, an enthusiastic proponent of rustic style who helped establish Yosemite National Park in 1894. Olmsted is perhaps most famous for designing New York's Central Park.

Log cabins were obviously appropriate for a region forested with straight, tall lodgepole pine, and it was logical to furnish these buildings with furniture that still looked like trees, plus occasional horn or antler pieces that trace their popularity back to the work of Texan Wenzel Friedrich in the 1880s. Railroads made it practical to import hickory furniture from the Indiana manufacturers. It wasn't until the rise of dude ranches in the 1910s and '20s through their glory days in the '30s and '40s, though, that there came a need for western furnishings with a hint of the romance of the Old West. This was, after all, what the dude ranches were selling. The new industry also created a market for western furnishings for vacationers who hoped to take a piece of the West home with them. Thus was born the beginning of what we now consider true western style.

Much of the work that resulted—from furniture makers like John Wurtz, Chet Woodward, Otto and Albert Nelson in Jackson, George Rathe in Montana, and from countless other cowhands and handymen who made furniture for their bosses in the cold, quiet winter months—was influenced by prevailing rustic styles. Resources included twigs and roots, horns and antlers of the hunting-lodge variety, and landscape materials from the immediate neighborhood—particularly lodgepole pine, willow, and driftwood.

As the designs and techniques matured and the flow of dudes and tourists increased, clever artisans drew on the symbols that had enchanted them in the first place: the tepees and beadwork of the Native Americans; the native wildlife such as buffalo, elk, deer, and bighorn sheep; the bucking horses, cattle, spurs, chaps, guns, and brands of the cowboy lifestyle; and the trees, rivers, and mountains of the surrounding landscape. The result was furniture from the land, with a nod to the region's history and the unmitigated use of romantic western symbols.

# The Development of Ranch Style

### A GUY NAMED MOLESWORTH

The "wrangler rustic," or "rustic western," or "cowboy high style," or "ranch" style of furniture will forever be associated with one man—Thomas Canada Molesworth. He did for western style what Buffalo Bill did for the West itself: by combining brilliant marketing with quality product, he bestowed on it lasting and indelible images that would forever be associated with the genre. Although others made furniture, none did it as long or as prolifically or with such flair.

A student at the Chicago Art Institute during the height of the American Arts & Crafts movement, Molesworth (1890–1977) founded the Shoshone Furniture Company in Cody, Wyoming, in 1931. By elevating functional ranch furniture to an art form, he defined western rustic style over the course of three decades. He applied leather, fringe, and brass tacks to desks, chairs, and dining room tables. He made chandeliers out of antlers, couches out of burls, and smoking stands out of hooves. He decorated beds, cabinets, and chair backs with painted, incised, or pierced images of cowboys, Indians, horses, and Rocky Mountain flowers and wildlife. Never afraid to take risks, Molesworth introduced vibrant yellow, lime green, and turquoise leather in understated ranch interiors, substituted bent deer legs for handles, and made sconces out of coyote heads. It goes without saying that he had a sense of humor.

"Lord knows, he made good furniture," says Mike Patrick, who knew Molesworth growing up, then went on to build Molesworth-inspired furniture. "His stuff is still in great shape. But he took everything to the absurd almost. You just had to see him giggling sometimes."

Says Wally Reber, a furniture maker and co-curator with Paul Fees of the 1989 Molesworth retrospective at the Buffalo Bill Historical Center in Cody, "He would take the fluted legs off a piano and replace them with pine legs, then he'd cover it with leather and brass heads and rope trim. He'd transform that thing from a piano to a Molesworth western rustic piano. His moose-antler wing chair [in which the 'wings' are the enormous antlers flaring out from the sides of a leather-and-pole easy chair], to me, was a humorous, genuinely gutsy piece. It was audacious."

Molesworth fulfilled commissions throughout

the West for hotels, dude ranches, and grand retreats modeled after the great camps of the Adirondacks. His furniture went east, too, to Dwight Eisenhower's study in Gettysburg and the display windows of Abercrombie & Fitch in New York City. For big commissions, Molesworth designed not just the furniture—from couches to magazine racks—but the entire space, from beaded curtains and painted lampshades to the Navajo rugs hanging from the beams.

*Thomas Canada Molesworth founded the Shoshone Furniture Company in Cody, Wyoming, in 1931. By elevating functional ranch furniture to an art form, he defined western rustic style over the course of three decades. For big commissions, he designed not just the furniture but the entire space, from the beaded curtains and painted lampshades to the Navajo rugs hanging from the beams. The result, seen here in a lodge in Jackson Hole, was furniture from the land, with a nod to the region's history and the unmitigated use of romantic western symbols.* Photo courtesy Mr. and Mrs. Lee Molesworth, Ventura, California.

"Molesworth was really a businessman and a designer," says Wally Reber, co-curator of the 1989 landmark exhibition on Molesworth at the Buffalo Bill Historical Center. "He was not a guy who spent his later years building furniture, but marketing, designing, assembling roomscapes, trading for Indian blankets, and reframing paintings. Molesworth was a man of the moment in a movement." The living room of the historic TE Ranch in Cody, Wyoming, was a fine example of Molesworth's ability to elevate functional ranch furniture to new heights of elegance. Photo courtesy Mr. and Mrs. Lee Molesworth, Ventura, California.

Says Reber, who examined hundreds of pieces of Molesworth furniture in preparation for the landmark exhibition, "The prevailing sense I had about it was its utter simplicity. From a pure furniture perspective, it wasn't exquisitely detailed. There weren't many mortise-and-tenon joints. The joinery was straightforward, and bolts were used a lot, which flies in the face of what's considered sophisticated. It was simply made but beautifully interpreted."

Rather, it was Molesworth's creative genius that was unusual, Reber continues. "The keyhole chair, with its round top and flared bottom, is not an unusual shape in any culture, but put in a western context, the chair became western. It never ceases to amaze me the kinds of interpretations that could be made on the back of the chairs, the incredible array of western motifs he was able to apply to such a pristine furniture element as a chair. Molesworth wasn't content to say, 'This is how I end all my chairs.' There were probably as many end pieces as there were clients. The form and construction were simple, but

the design and creation were very elegant."

While the furniture's designs exhibited enormous artistic flair, function was never overlooked. Across the country, entire roomscapes have withstood the abuse of more than five decades. At ranches throughout the West, his couches and chairs have nobly served the gatherings that attend ranch life, with their inevitable muddy boots, wet dogs, generations of rambunctious children, and even the occasional orphaned lamb.

"Some of it was a little humorous, some quite different," says Lee Molesworth, who during his childhood often worked in his father's shop after school. "But a lot of it was practical designs that fit into the lifestyle of the people it was for. I think he thought he was creating something that would fit into the western theme. Of course," he adds, "he had furniture in just about every state in the union."

*Molesworth fulfilled commissions throughout the West for hotels, dude ranches, and grand retreats modeled after the great camps of the Adirondacks. The Grand Hotel in Billings, Montana, was one such commission. His furniture went east, too, to Dwight Eisenhower's study in Gettysburg and the display windows of Abercrombie & Fitch in New York City.* Photo courtesy Mr. and Mrs. Lee Molesworth, Ventura, California.

## REINVENTING MOLESWORTH

Fashion inevitably changes with time. Molesworth closed his shop in 1958, and while his furniture serves its mission well to this day, by the 1960s, western rustic furniture had faded from favor. Locals looked to both coasts and abroad for a sense of what was fashion forward, while absentee ranch owners and visiting dudes regarded the Molesworth furniture they came into contact with as quaint regional folk art at best, and pure kitsch at worst.

*Molesworth did not turn up his artistic nose at commissions, such as this set of furniture for a man whose main civic activity was membership in the Shriners. "Some of it was a little humorous, some quite different," says Lee Molesworth, who, during his childhood, often worked in his father's shop after school. "But a lot of it was practical designs that fit into the lifestyle of the people it was for."* Photo courtesy Mr. and Mrs. Lee Molesworth, Ventura, California.

Molesworth furniture languished in obscurity for a few decades until Paul Fees and Wally Reber of the Buffalo Bill Historical Center in Cody got interested in this homegrown Frank Lloyd Wright of the Rockies.

"In Cody in the 1980s," Reber recalls, "you would go from professional building to professional building and from someone's house to someone's house, and you'd see this interesting furniture made by a guy named Molesworth. I

wanted to find out more, but it wasn't easy. The more I looked into it, the bigger the question became. Many, many people thought it was odd furniture and wanted to get rid of it. On the other hand, some were so enchanted by it they didn't want anyone else to know about it. It was far enough out of fashion that if one had been shrewd, one could have cornered the market on it. We heard horror stories of people burning it or selling it at garage sales."

The result was an exhibition that opened at the Buffalo Bill Historical Center in 1989, then traveled to the Gene Autry Museum in Los Angeles the following year. "It struck a chord," Mike Patrick says simply.

More than that, it launched a cycle of awareness and appreciation for Molesworth furniture

*A conference-room suite of Molesworth reproductions made by Sweetwater Ranch from original Molesworth patterns showcases the cowboy high style Molesworth's name became synonymous with: huge burls and applied half-poles, colored leather and brass tacks, cut-metal chandeliers, and the famous cowboy-silhouette keyhole chair.* Photo © Dewey Vanderhoff.

specifically and rustic ranch furniture in general that continues to escalate. Furniture once relegated to the attic now sits on the auction block at Christie's. Regional craftsmen, whether exposed to the work for the first time or simply seeing familiar work from a fresh perspective, were drawn to the style just as visitors, ranch owners, and longtime locals discovered how beautifully it met their needs. The exhibit helped establish the western rustic genre as firmly as Adirondack and southwestern had been established decades before as distinctive, identifiable schools of design; in doing so, it opened the door to the legion of contemporary western furniture makers working today.

In the decade since the show, those craftspeople and their work have evolved to represent an extraordinary breadth of creative vision and work-manship where quality goes hand-in-hand with aesthetics. While their creativity, their embracing of natural forms and materials, and their relentless drive for quality goes well beyond what Molesworth ever did, they certainly owe an enormous debt to one man's vision.

Reber reflects, "Molesworth really was as big as all outdoors. He had a mind that allowed him to pursue furniture differently than it had been done before. He was very sophisticated. And he was the juice behind the movement."

# Contemporary Expressions of the West

### FROM THE HEART OF THE LAND

**K**en Siggins's workshop sits in the shadow of Wyoming's Absaroka Mountains, in the spectacular upper valley of the South Fork of the Shoshone River. There, he has been building western furniture since 1964, first for his parents' dude ranch and the guests who stayed there, then for the people who flocked to Cody from all over the country when Molesworth's work was rediscovered.

"In the early days of western furniture building," he recalls, "you had to make your own market. A lot of my early clients were people who came out to the ranch and wanted to take a little piece of the West home with them. My grandfather had made furniture for the ranch; it was Adirondack influenced—posts and rails done with a drawknife. I grew up around Molesworth's furniture. It was all around town—in doctors' offices, the auditorium." Years later, when the museum launched a retrospective of Molesworth's work, Siggins says, "I really did think the show was a credible thing to do. Then the *New York Times* and the *Wall Street Journal* said, 'This is a big thing.' And it was off and running."

"At first only several hundred people in the country were interested in this furniture," recalls Lester Santos, who worked on Molesworth furniture for Sweetwater Ranch before striking out to build his own designs. "Now there are people who have never seen it before—and they're ordering it. People contact me through my Website from England and other countries, and I think, 'Where are they coming from?'"

The answer's not complicated. Western furniture is a tangible representation of those elements of the West that have struck a chord since Buffalo Bill Cody first took his Wild West Show across the ocean more than a century ago. As such, it resonates not just with homeowners in the American West but also with anyone who has a hankering for wide-open spaces, pure country air, and a desire to get closer to nature. Furniture built with natural materials brings the outside in, whether you live in Cheyenne or Chicago.

"Western furniture provides a vicarious experience of the West that makes people feel good," points out Mike Patrick. A vigorous promoter of the western school of design, Patrick is an environmentalist and proponent of sustainable

development who believes that our ongoing love affair with the West is both a curse and a blessing. "It's filling up our meadows with people, and it's diminishing our wildlife because everyone wants a piece of it. But I think it's inevitable. However, we can use landscape-friendly development and destination tourism as a vehicle for the kinds of sustainable economic development that the West needs to maintain healthy communities."

While the loss of elk habitat to twenty-acre

*Meticulous craftsmanship and new ways of handling traditional materials are two main qualities distinguishing the fine work coming out of today's West.*
Photo: David O. Marlow.

ranchettes is certainly a concern, he acknowledges that newcomers sustain a market for craftspeople; the growth supports many families in regionally significant traditional livelihoods who might otherwise be forced to work at Wal-Mart. The work of these artisans, in turn, helps sustain the region's

*Western furniture always speaks to the land. It resonates with anyone who yearns for wide-open spaces, pure country air, and a desire to get closer to nature.*
Photo by Kay Lynn Reilly.

distinct identity at a time when growth is making it more homogeneous, threatening the West with the loss of its unique regional flavor.

Today, scores of western craftspeople work from garages and cabins and woodshops and old barns throughout the West (and in some not-so-western places like Wisconsin, New York, and Kentucky). While some use production-line construction methods, the overriding majority are serious woodworkers, metalworkers, leatherworkers, bead workers, and ceramicists who work alone or with a spouse, partner, or apprentice. They work on each piece from start to finish, from the first conceptual talks with a client to the day the piece is delivered in the backs of their trucks. Many gather all their materials by hand, roaming the backcountry, riverbanks, and foothills for gnarly burls, pristine antlers, dead-standing juniper,

beautifully colored willow, and intriguingly shaped driftwood. They tread lightly on the land and abhor waste. They spend countless hours sanding, shaping, and simply letting the wood speak to them. Their inspiration comes from the land.

## THE FREE EDGE OF NATURE

The overwhelming impression of this body of work as a whole is meticulous craftsmanship applied to a constantly evolving definition of what is western. The process is driven by the increasingly sophisticated eye of the craftsperson and his or her unique artistic influences and vision.

"In western furniture, there are no simple labels, but we used to see a lot of reproductions, a lot of distressed furniture, a lot of fish and buffalo heads on poles," says Bob Brown, whose Big Horn Gallery in Cody has represented furniture as fine art for more than a decade. "Now we see the introduction of different woods. A lot of people got away from pine, for instance; and juniper—although it had always been used—is now being used differently. The forms have become less rigid; pieces have become more curved, more free-flowing," a process craftsman Lester Santos calls "moving toward the free edge of nature."

"Ten years ago," Brown continues, "it was obvious right out of the gate that people were doing Molesworth reproductions, making pole furniture, and attempting to duplicate what he had succeeded with. And the buyers were looking for Molesworth reproductions. After a while, though, the craftspeople began to develop their own styles, creative works that took Molesworth one step beyond. Then the buyers began to realize there were people doing more creative things."

Kentucky craftsman Dan MacPhail's creativity, for instance, emboldened him to build a Christmas tree out of elk antlers. The resulting piece is remarkable for its balance and symmetry, presenting a surprising dignity that absolutely defies kitsch. MacPhail's leather armchair with moose antlers incorporates the antlers structurally along its sides; fine craftsmanship creates a seamless marriage of leather and antlers. Despite the length and curve of the antlers, the leather has not one wrinkle; viewed from the back, the chair resembles fingers gently cupping a baby's bottom.

A constant striving toward meticulous craftsmanship allows for old ideas to be used in new ways, such as Chris Chapman's unique handling of leather, in which the leather is worked—pressed, kneaded, and persuaded—into a pattern, rather than tooled. Jim and Lynda Covert combined his driftwood-inspired furniture with her

*New western designers work on each piece from start to finish, from the first conceptual talks with a client to the day they deliver the pieces from the backs of their trucks. Many gather all their materials by hand, roaming the backcountry, riverbanks, and foothills for gnarly burls, pristine antlers, intriguingly shaped driftwood, beautifully colored willow, and the sculptural forms of dead-standing juniper.* Photo by Roger Toll.

lifelong interest in Plains Indian beadwork; they applied beaded panels to the sides of some Molesworth-style club chairs, to stunning effect. "Molesworth went to great lengths to find new things to do," Lynda points out. "It's a natural progression for us Revivalists."

*Contemporary artisans are following their muse and allowing the materials themselves to dictate the forms, as in this remarkable "Anti-Gravity" table from New West Furniture. "The end result is great," says Marty Kruzich, of Martin-Harris Gallery in Jackson, Wyoming, "but it's the process that's so fascinating."*
Photo courtesy of the artist.

Western design has matured, and with this maturity comes work that is increasingly better crafted, belying its longtime reputation as crude and primitive. "The bottom line," says Wally Reber, "is that western furniture has very rapidly become much more sophisticated in its construction, its finish applications, its materials, and its interpretation."

Marty Kruzich, partner in the Martin-Harris

Gallery in Jackson, Wyoming, has witnessed this evolution in quality firsthand; the gallery has been showing furniture as fine art for thirteen years. When Kruzich speaks of these artisans' work, his tone is reverential.

"Dana Merrill pulls wood from the earth, scrapes off 100 years of soil, wood, and animal crud but leaves blemishes—the mark of a nail or a scratch from a container or a hole that had been eroded—and turns it into the most incredible work, with vintage pulls and hardware and tiny pieces of cut glass. James Howard, who lives in Long Lake, New York, makes the most incredible furniture because he has all winter to make it. He walks around the lake looking for pieces;

*A visit to a craftsman's workshop, such as the antler-rich studio at Crystal Farm Antler Chandeliers, is a visual and tactile experience that speaks of the timelessness of the contemporary West.* Photo courtesy of the artist.

he throws nails with the wrong patina into the woodstove, then picks through the ashes for them. Brad Greenwood does some of the best design work you'll ever find. He uses the wood to its strongest advantage in his composition and never lets you forget that it was once a tree. Don King is a chair maker who'll walk fifty miles to find just the right piece of wood to match a particular chair. He's like a sculptor; his wood dictates the piece. His chairs are what music would look like if you could see it."

## ONCE A TREE

For many of these craftspeople, their craft is a calling, an inevitability as well as a lifestyle decision. Ron Shanor was working in a mechanized shop, in a job so mindless he was reading a 300-page book every day. When his boss told him he couldn't read on the job anymore, he quit and started making furniture. In the early days he sold his work out of the back of his truck. Several years ago, his wife, Jean, injured herself sanding and faced the prospect of having to give up her work in the shop. "The specter of having to work at Wal-Mart just freaked me out," she recalls. So she built a highly detailed miniature cabin as an art piece, sold it, and has been making them ever since. The Shanors periodically head into the mountains to hunt for the heavy burls that are their work's signature, all of which they gather themselves from three or four sites around Wyoming. "Getting into the mountains," Ron admits, "is one of the best parts of the job."

For these artisans, it's all about a way of life, and the chosen lifestyle informs the work, Kruzich says. "Thome George and Cloudbird are home-schooling, carrying their own water, and being treed by wildcats as they scout the roots for their furniture. They can only work certain hours of the day because they have no electricity. They're passionate about what they do. They have a muse that demands perfection. Jack Moseley makes lamps at 11,000 feet in Colorado where the only things that move are the clouds being pushed by the wind. He takes dead-standing juniper and carves a lampshade and base from it, and you'd swear it still breathes."

The common denominator in new western design is the pursuit of an ideal; that ideal combines technical prowess with a striving for beauty within an expanded western vernacular. For those who are lucky enough to live with this furniture, says Washington State craftsman Thome George, it becomes a "sea anchor" in a tempestuous world, a tangible icon of both nature and the freedom that the West represents. Photo © Elijah Cobb.

These artisans practice the Zen of furniture making, pursuing an absolute passion. "Most of these artists would do it for no other reason than to do it," says Kruzich. "They realize they might make more as a night clerk, but they can't *not* do it. Mark Koons takes wood from construction-site dumpsters because he can't stand the thought of it being thrown away. He brings it home and stacks it, and it takes him a year to make one piece. Someone asked him, 'Why do you do it?' He said, 'I can't answer that question. I have to do it.'"

The pieces that result from this extraordinary commitment, Kruzich continues, "have a soul, have been nurtured in their development, have gone through gestation, and have been born, like a child. Believe it or not, the craftsmen want their pieces to go to good homes. They ask, 'Are the people nice?'"

*The use of natural materials from the landscape—and found objects from old barns and farmyards—brings the outside in, whether you live in Cheyenne or Chicago, and speaks to the cultural history of the region.*
Photo © Dewey Vanderhoff.

# Into the Future

## QUINTESSENTIALLY WESTERN

Just as contemporary westerners are the product of myriad cultural influences ranging from ancient Native American tribes and Spanish-descended Mexicans to settlers from Scandinavia and Asian railroad workers, so the furniture of the contemporary West is the product of an array of aesthetic influences. From the original rustic—Adirondack and North Woods mosaic twig work and bark, and Indiana hickory—to the clean lines of the Arts & Crafts movement, from Victorian to the Southwest, from Mission to Monterey, western furniture is difficult to pigeonhole. Yet, in all its manifestations, through its basic forms and materials it remains quintessentially western.

Western pop artist Bill Schenck and his business partner Steve Alverson's Molesworth Revival furniture, for instance, combines highly stylized southwestern images with art deco elements. Lately they've been playing with Queen Anne style and have introduced steel to pueblo style. "We're bringing together different types of furniture that have been around for centuries and trying to marry these influences," says Alverson.

*Meticulous craftsmanship combined with indigenous materials and traditional subject matter, as in this desk by Jim Covert with cast-bronze work by artist Peter Fillerup, are the hallmarks of contemporary western furniture.* Photo courtesy of the artist.

Rather than a haphazard attempt to simply come up with something new, contemporary designs are conceived in a marriage of intellect, artistry, and historical precedent. "We can expand the definition way beyond what Molesworth and Paul Hindman ever did," asserts Bill Schenck, "and still stay within the tradition of that style of furniture. Our approach is to put it in historical context; we have a very clear idea of where we want to go that's separate and different from what other people are doing. But the end object is still that the furniture has to be totally elegant as well as functional."

To be western, it also has to speak to the land. Inspiration can be far ranging if the result

*The furniture of the contemporary West is the product of an array of aesthetic influences. From Victorian to Southwestern, from Mission to Monterey, western furniture is difficult to pigeonhole. Recent manifestations may look for their inspiration as far afield as art deco and Queen Anne, yet they remain, through their basic forms and materials, quintessentially western. "We can expand the definition of western," says artist and designer Bill Schenck, "and still stay within the tradition of that style of furniture. We have a very clear idea of where we want to go that's separate and different from what other people are doing, but the end object is still that the furniture has to be totally elegant as well as functional."* Photo © Jack Kotz.

feels at home in the West. Ron and Jean Shanor, enamored of the Victorian era, will make a table lamp from a burl base, then top it with a rawhide lampshade given a Victorian look with a "fringe" of tiny burls dangling from its edges. New West Furniture has been exploring the fertile ground in their Stickley-esque Morris chair, westernized with the use of pine in place of quarter-sawn oak and trimmed with whipstitched leather upholstery. Norwegian Reidar Wahl scours new and out-of-print books for antique southwestern pieces, selectively picking up details he might incorporate into his contemporary, made-to-look-old, Scandinavian-influenced furniture. Closer to home, stylistically speaking, Ken Siggins incorporates an Adirondack influence

*Across the Mountain West, old homesteaders' cabins—such as this one-room cabin rebuilt on its original site east of Yellowstone and turned into an office—are being refurbished by people wanting to retain a connection to the region's history. Hand-built furnishings are often the only appropriate choice for these structures.* Photo © 2000 Chase Reynolds Ewald.

in his decidedly Molesworth-inspired pieces.

"Everyone has their own historic version of what things used to be," points out Greg Race, whose intensely intellectual approach applies cutting-edge techniques and material treatments to traditional forms. "The Victorian influence was probably more a component of the American West than ranching and mining. But some people's definition of western is attached to rustic."

[ 34 ]

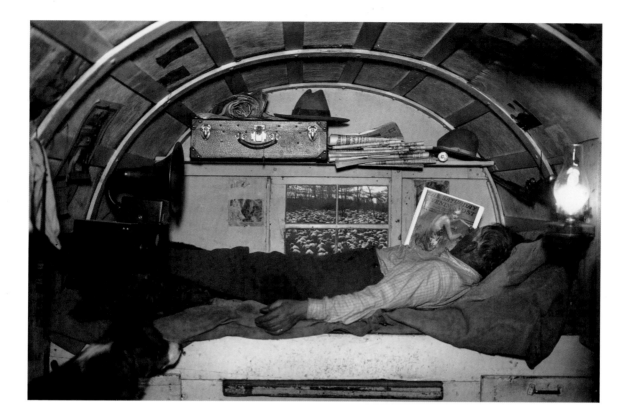

Deadly serious about their craft they may be, but there's always a place for humor, an important commodity in a land where resources are scarce. There's no shortage of it in the work of contemporary western craftspeople. They're not afraid to have fun with their furniture, whether it's New West's bed made from irrigation pipes with "linens" of orange ditch cloth and Carhart overalls, or Wally Reber's teacart in the shape of a buffalo. A healthy dose of whimsy and nostalgia are in play as well, from Anne Beard's upholstered ottomans bearing the likeness of a 1930s cowgirl hugging her horse to L. D. Burke's one-of-a-kind pieces with inscribed or applied sayings ("When the going gets tough, the tough go fishing") that leap into his mind unbidden, often in the middle of the night.

*Despite the rise of log mansions, there are many who still feel that less is more. Sheepherder wagons today are being pressed into service as guest rooms and fishing shacks as quickly as they're retired from active duty.* Photo courtesy Buffalo Bill Historical Center, Cody, WY, Charles Belden Collection.

## INTO THE MILLENNIUM

Just as Buffalo Bill shipped his vision of the West across continents and oceans, western furniture is not necessarily staying in the West, nor is it always destined for log cabins. Brad Greenwood's work is in the East and Midwest, with a fair number of pieces in contemporary homes. Leslie Northrup says many of her mirrors hang in friends' apartments in New York City, where they bring a slice of the Big Sky to cramped quarters.

The common denominator in new western design is the pursuit of an ideal; that ideal combines technical prowess with a striving for beauty within an expanded western vernacular. For craftsman Lester Santos, beauty is at its most pure in nature. "When I go to look for wood," he says, "I see dead

*Wyoming craftsman Lester Santos started his furniture-making career following the forms established by legendary furniture maker Thomas Molesworth but has since evolved his own style, which celebrates the natural beauty and organic forms of juniper, as in this chandelier. Western craftspeople today are letting go of traditional forms and moving toward what Santos calls "the free edge of nature."* Photo © Elijah Cobb.

junipers that are gorgeous works of art just standing in the ground. It's hard to improve on a tree."

"The most important thing to me," Santos continues, "is how my furniture makes people feel, whether the designs actually move people or not. I had a client who saw one of my small painted chairs in a gallery and started to cry. Then she purchased it. I want my furniture to communicate my feelings."

Comments Debbie Hindman, an interior designer in Denver, "These craftspeople are creating things that are timeless and a hundred years from now will be antiques. They'll be around because they're incredibly well made, not just beautiful. And that's something that people sometimes don't understand. This furniture is worlds apart; it's meant to exist for a lifetime, or ten."

For those who are lucky enough to live with this furniture, says Thome George, it becomes a "sea anchor" in a tempestuous world, a tangible icon of both nature and the freedom the West represents in a fast-forward, digitized culture. For the craftspeople who make it, the furniture is their vocation and their avocation, an artistic expression of self. Simply put, it's a way of life.

*New western design must speak to the world outside the door without distracting from it. "The thing you have to get in your mind,"* says Debbie Hindman of *the design firm Associates III in Denver, "is that the interiors can't compete with the views."* Photo © 2000 Chase Reynolds Ewald.

# First Impressions

### ENTRYWAYS

Whatever the setting, a home's style extends as far as its front gate or driveway entrance, where the address might be identified by an imposing log archway complete with a cut-metal silhouette of the ranch brand. Or it may be noted by nothing more than the red numbered highway marker mandated by the post office on rural routes. But whether the western home is a weekend refuge in a crowded resort area, a suburban home, or a working ranch, the front door is where a tone is set, where the outside world falls away. There, one crosses a threshold both literally and figuratively.

A sense of arrival is established at the outset through a home's architecture, entryway layout, and plantings. Graceful touches are achieved through the use of handcrafted elements, whether it's bent-willow porch furniture flanking the doorway, whimsical driftwood birds hanging overhead, a striking hand-carved door, or a hand-cut lighting fixture above glass doors with a bold, warm and welcoming red framework.

The front door itself may speak volumes about the people who live behind it. On one Wyoming

ranch, a heavy handcrafted door of chip-carved walnut is inset with a framework of applied juniper sticks. The twig work encases two hand-carved panels, one featuring a grizzly bear, the other an owl, both of which are spotted frequently on the property and in the surrounding national forest. The bear's paw prints—two front and two back—seem to lead the visitor inside, as if to say "Follow me."

The entryway of another home that serves as headquarters of a working ranch north of Yellowstone alludes to both its ranch lifestyle and the region's history. Instead of a grand entry hall, one enters a practical, no-nonsense mudroom. Its inglenook seating and wooden wainscoting hearken back to a time when the Arts & Crafts movement was at its peak, an era that coincided with the settlement of Montana. Cowboy hats and lariats take the place of formal artwork to create a living work that changes from day to day. Exposed wood glows with an inviting warmth, and the human scale of the space allows for a sense of opening up as one enters the great room beyond.

Even when the front door opens directly into the heart of the home, it is possible to create a distinctive first impression. One northern Rockies abode sets its tone with a remarkable floor that

The owner and designer of this home, built by Alpine Log Homes on a working ranch outside Oklahoma City, says visitors are surprised to see logs in this region. The logs have been coated with a gray wash to help withstand Oklahoma's extreme weather conditions and trimmed with a cheerful, welcoming red. A handcrafted lighting fixture by Tony Alvis illuminates the front entry.

Photo © 2000 David Fitzgerald & Associates.

*The new Snow Lodge at Old Faithful in Yellowstone National Park heralds the beginning of a new western aesthetic for the park service. Guests arriving at the striking building are treated to lighting fixtures both inside and outside that were created by New York craftsman Steve Blood, whose father did marquetry work for Thomas Molesworth.* Photo © 2000 Chase Reynolds Ewald.

features an inset panel of cross-sectioned fir log ends embedded in pea gravel then set with polyurethane for durability. The log ends suggest the surrounding forests; the tiny stones represent the streambeds for which Montana is famous. Says architect Van Bryan, of Apogee Architects in Bozeman, "It sets the stage and indicates that there will be interesting surprises throughout the house."

One home in the cattle and wheat-raising country near Oklahoma City surprises the visitor through its architecture. Here, log homes are uncommon, even on working ranches. A gray wash on the logs serves as protection from the extremes of weather on the open plains while ton-

ing down the lodgelike flavor. Inside, however, there's nothing subtle about the homeowner's passion for the West. Bold western artwork and handcrafted furnishings extend throughout the house: a horse-and-rider-motif lighting fixture hangs over the entryway, and leather-topped tables, cowhide couches, fringed leather curtains, and cast-bronze chandeliers with Indians mounted on galloping horses are scattered throughout the house. A longhorn head over the fireplace refers to the animals grazing outside, while cast-bronze buffalo on the chandeliers have their own living counterparts on the property.

A western home doesn't have to be in the mountains to speak to its surroundings. And sometimes it's more relaxing to surround yourself with imagery rather than the real thing. Buffalo, for instance, are difficult to care for, notes the homeowner. "We don't have too many," she says, "because they don't want to stay inside the fence for long."

*An entry designed by Annette Stelmack of Associates III in Denver, Colorado, makes clever use of a door within a door, which opens invitingly into a room featuring a chandelier crafted by Crystal Farm Antler Chandeliers and a Tiffany lamp set atop a Taos drum.* Photo: David O. Marlow.

[ 41 ]

A career as a sawyer in the backwoods of Kentucky prepared Jim Covert well for the work he pursues with wood today. Covert's furniture is identifiable from a distance for its organic, beautifully balanced design and wonderfully grained wood that glows from within. Covert is a purist whose noncommercial instincts free him to take several months off a year gathering inspiration in the deep woods of Canada, the Appalachian hardwood forests of Indiana, and the unpeopled mountains of Wyoming. His uncompromising pursuit of perfection guarantees him more customers than he can handle, putting him in the enviable position of accepting only commissions that truly intrigue him.

A king-sized bed with a footboard compartment for a television? "That doesn't really interest me." Twin beds for three-year-old twin girls? "I've never done little girl beds," he muses. "I've done little boy beds but not little girl beds." The project is simpler than most of his work, befitting the subjects, but he follows his inspiration and surprises the clients by carving the girls' initials flanked by rising eagles in the footboards of the beds.

The more complex pieces , however, are what Covert is known for: the classic Morris-chair form in richly colored

*Dogs are as ubiquitous as welcome mats in the West.* Photo © 2000 Chase Reynolds Ewald.

applied pole inset with one-of-a-kind hand-beaded leather panels made by his wife, Lynda; a massive dining room table situated atop a fantastically curved juniper stump that has been meticulously worked to bring out its color, grain, and character; an upright desk with inset leather, hand-forged drawer pulls by sculptor Peter Fillerup, and a secret drawer cleverly hidden underneath.

Covert began his career as a furniture maker in 1984 when he joined forces with Cody craftsman Ken

Siggins. Things were slow in the western furniture business at that time but that gave Covert time to make the transition to master woodworker. After a few lean years, fortune smiled on them. "When people started to discover Molesworth, they'd come to Cody and ask for furniture and the Chamber of Commerce sent them to us." Even before the Molesworth exhibition, they were doing jobs for New York architects and high-profile designers, and they worked to make sure their quality stayed even with expectations.

Covert and Siggins continued to collaborate on large projects, but by 1992 Covert had established Covert Workshops and made a name with his distinctive driftwood furniture. "The problem, though, was that it took so long to find all the right pieces. I'd look at a couple thousand pieces a day and only pick up fifty. It was physically and mentally exhausting." Eventually, he recalls, "I was wanting to introduce some refinement to western furniture; I wanted to get some elegance going. One way to do that is in the material, by making sure the material has some dignity and integrity. So I started using cherry and walnut with driftwood and juniper, and it really worked well."

Meanwhile, Covert's wife, Lynda,

had mastered the art of leatherwork and upholstery. Raised near the Sioux country of South Dakota, she had grown up practicing beadwork. The couple introduced beaded leather side panels on Molesworth-style armchairs to much acclaim. Soon, Lynda was also offering curtains, blankets, pillows, and other items of intricately beaded designs on sumptuous leathers. The two still collaborate on many projects, and Jimmy also incorporates carved-wood or cast-bronze panels by other artists.

"I try not to take on too much work. I want to steal back some of my exploratory time," says Covert. "I still have lots to learn. I'm always trying to make that perfect thing, and it's going to be a lifelong pursuit."

*A heavy door is necessary to stand up to Wyoming winds. This one is of chip-carved walnut inset within a framework of applied juniper sticks by master craftsman Jim Covert. The twig work encases two panels hand carved by Blackfoot Oneida Indian Rod Skenandore, one featuring a grizzly bear, the other an owl—both of which are spotted frequently on the 7,000-acre working ranch. The grizzly bear's paw prints seem to lead the visitor inside, as if to say, "Come on in."* Photo © 2000 Chase Reynolds Ewald.

At the foot of the Los Padres Mountains and overlooking the Santa Barbara Channel lies the workshop of metalworker Tony Alvis. "This part of California is where the *vaqueros* came from; the word *buckaroo* came from *vaquero*," says Alvis. "This is where bits and spurs were made by the missions. Here, horsemanship was developed to an art. This is where they roped grizzly bears. My shop and horses are on one of the old mission land grants." Ancient adobes abound, the Spanish influence is palpable, and the region boasts some of the best horse trainers and rodeo competitors in the country.

It is no wonder, then, that this master blacksmith turned his metalwork toward art, becoming a leading metalsmith in a genre that is rapidly becoming crowded.

Alvis's first piece—suggested while contemplating his own mounted silhouette with a string of pack mules behind him—was not without precedent, he says. "I'd been working in steel and with horseshoes as a blacksmith and I'd seen a lot of this type of work around here. I have old brochures from the 1920s with tons of those scenes on weathervanes and matchbook holders and candleholders. I just started making my own things. I started cutting out in detail.

Most of this type of work is generic looking or plain. When I cut out, you can see the light shining through and the muscle tone on the cowboys."

In addition to his art-metalwork, he does ranch work, takes dudes into the backcountry, furnishes mules for the Forest Service, and does his own farrier work.

He grew up between Pasadena and Los Angeles on the Arroyo Seco, a mecca for devotees of the Arts & Crafts movement. "I love the Arts & Crafts period," he says. "I grew up with the Mission style and the Greene & Greene influence. The Southwest Indian Museum was right down the street; it was one of the best Indian museums in the country. And there were a lot of homes around built out of riverbed rock. The old horse trails went right through the area and we lived next to the parks that line the old freeway. I didn't know I lived near a city."

All these influences come together seamlessly in Alvis's work. Starting with sheets of steel, he explains, "You just work it. I pound the hell out of it. My elbows kill me at the end of the day. It's hard on the body, but I want to give it a real textured look so it looks old. A lot of people think my pieces *are* old."

Fireplace screens are a staple: classic

Photo © Alan Hagman.

western scenes of mounted cowboys over-looking a saguaro-cactus desert, or wilderness and wildlife tableaux, or the occasional oceanscape. "If you have a good fireplace screen, the interplay of flickering light behind the silhouette is so fascinating," he says.

Large chandeliers offer a challenge and complexity beyond the flat surface of the fireplace screen, and outdoor lighting fixtures are four-sided canvases. Alvis also makes the occasional still life, such as an eight-foot grizzly bear standing on its hind legs. "Sometimes when I'm in between jobs, I just want to make something different. I can't stand to make the same thing over and over." A particularly unusual commission was a spiral staircase of iron featuring two cowboys pushing a herd of cattle down a mountain.

Metalwork comes naturally to Alvis, who studied the western art of Charlie Russell, Frederic Remington, and Jo Mora voraciously, and history affects him vividly. "Blacksmiths run in my family," he discovered recently. "There were blacksmiths back in my great-great-great-grandfathers' time. It gave me chills when I found out my grandfathers were blacksmiths."

*A cut-metal lamp by California craftsman Tony Alvis lights the way to an artist's studio made by builder Chris Taylor in Wapiti, Wyoming, from a hundred-year-old building original to the property.* Photo © 2000 Chase Reynolds Ewald.

The soaring space that is this home's main entry hall combines a massive yet graceful antler chandelier, western bronzes, a hand-carved door from India, and a slab of petrified wood hung as art. Photo © 2000 Elijah Cobb.

Hardware is a subtle but important detail in a home; the doorknob is one's first tactile experience of a house. Rocky Mountain Hardware's handmade bronze handle mimics the branches outside the window. Photo © Jerry Hadam Photography.

In many western homes, one enters directly into the heart of the living area. One northern Rockies entry sets its distinctive tone with a remarkable floor featuring an inset panel of cross-sectioned fir log ends set in pea gravel and then filled in with polyurethane for durability. The log ends rereerence the surrounding forests while the tiny stones represent the streambeds for which Montana is famous. Says architect Van Bryan of Apogee Architects in Bozeman, "It sets the stage and indicates that there will be interesting surprises throughout the house." Photo © 2000 Lynn Donaldson.

Jerry Wayne Bement (alias J. Dub's) traveled through the mountain states as a farrier for a number of years before settling in Ellensburg, Washington, in 1980. A chance request by a friend to make a weathervane (of a dog jumping over the moon) showed Bement that his true calling was that of an artist-craftsman. Having no formal art training, he followed his instincts, using photographs and tracing paper as aids, but relied on his intuition for proportion, composition, and artistry. In 1989, he entered his first crafts fair at the Ellensburg Rodeo "just to see if there was any interest." Despite selling nothing the first day, "everyone said they'd never seen anything like it," Bement recalls. Then he appeared at the Pikes Place Market as well as the Bellevue Arts Festival, which attracts buyers from around the country with its 600 juried participants. Articles in *Esquire* and other publications generated over a thousand inquiries. By the time the Eddie Bauer catalog came knocking at his door, he was positioned to expand even further, adding more employees and generally gearing up to become a production home-furnishings operation. Then one day he noticed he wasn't the only one doing silhouette images anymore.

"I was all ready to get into production mode," he recalls, "and I went into a custom mode instead. Now I'm pretty much a one-man band." And that suits him. Working in stainless steel, bronze, mild steel, and brass (mostly cut but some hammered), Bement specializes in fireplace screens and balcony panels but also makes chandeliers and even some furniture. He layers different metals for a three-dimensional look and uses accents of contrasting metals as highlights. His imagery tends to be western—horses among aspens, cowboys and Indians, wildlife and mountainscapes. He's also one for humor: a cowboy astride a bucking salmon, for instance, was popular back when he was selling to tourists. His portrayal of horses reveals a career spent working closely with these animals and an intimate knowledge of their body language evident in the arch of a neck or the flick of a foal's tail. He's not afraid of complexity; the sixteen-foot-long *Wyoming* image combines mountains, trees, and thirty-four distinct birds and animals. His signature image, *Thirty Cowboys,* is best suited for a gateway where width is no object: the cowboy-hatted riders, each distinct but all moving toward the viewer, span a twenty-foot distance, allowing plenty of clearance for a gooseneck trailer.

Photo courtesy of the artist.

Bement pulls a portable shop—outfitted with a heater and exhaust fans, a welder and power source, drill presses, grinders, air compressors, and a plasma cutter (which easily cuts bronze, brass, aluminum, and steel)—behind his truck. This allows him to work on-site and collaborate with the client. It also facilitates his taking artistic inspiration from each setting, using its particular mountainscapes, local flora and fauna, even a silhouette of a distinctive tree, as in a piece with two enormous cedar trees on Whidbey Island in Puget Sound. A commission in the upper Midwest, where, he says, "they're just starting to come into the log-home look," involved four fireplace screens and a thirty-foot-long balcony panel. A job in Pagosa Springs, Colorado, consisted of sixteen fireplace screens located in five buildings.

"It's been crazy ever since that first crafts fair in 1989," Bement says. "I've never been able to get caught up."

A glimpse of wagon wheel, a bleached skull against logs:
these are classic elements that make a room western.
Photo © 2000 Chase Reynolds Ewald.

A slab-and-branch bench by Montana woodworker Rob Mazza
sounds an artistic note against a palette of wood
and white. Photo courtesy of the artist.

*The entryway of a Montana home refers to its ranch lifestyle and the region's history, a theme that is carried through-out the house. Rather than a grand entry hall, one enters a practical, no-nonsense mudroom. Its inglenook seating and wooden wainscoting hearken back to a time when the Arts & Crafts movement was at its height, an era that coincided with the settlement of Montana.* Photo © 2000 Lynn Donaldson.

# Family Spaces

## LIVING ROOMS

The hearth of the home is indeed the heart of the home—and nowhere more so than in the West, where references to the outdoors and the simpler lifestyle of the past are ubiquitous. The two come together in the work of a growing number of sculptors and metal artisans who design intricately made fireplace screens for homes throughout the West. The meticulously cut or sculpted images speak to the region's scenery, wildlife, cowboy heritage, Native American history, and outdoor pursuits.

"If you've ever sat out in the woods in front of a crackling fire," muses Utah artist Peter Fillerup, "one of the things you do is stare into the fire, and your imagination goes in all different directions. All we're doing with fireplace screens is pulling some of those romantic images out. Each image tells a story."

Familiar mountainscapes—bugling bull elk bearing enormous antler racks; cowboys with lariats aloft, chasing cattle; mounted Indians, bows pulled back, aiming for buffalo; fishermen attempting to reel in leaping trout—all come alive through the play of firelight. Backlit by the dancing flames, the images bring a slice of wilderness right into the living room.

As the living room centers around the fireplace, so the house centers on the western living room or great room. The challenges inherent in dealing with this kind of space include balancing the grand vistas outside with the interior space, making soaring rooms feel cozy, and adding warmth and texture to the typical exposed wood and stone surfaces. Homeowners seek varying degrees of western flavor, but virtually all desire comfort and functionality.

"Our lifestyle is changing, not just here but everywhere," comments Lynn Harker of Harker Design. "It's nice to have a piece of furniture you can put your feet up on."

"The style is much more casual than what we've seen in the past," agrees Debbie Hindman of Denver design firm Associates III. "Our clients want to be able to get off their horses and put their boots up on the coffee table."

*Thomas Molesworth meets Molesworth-inspired in this original end table paired with a burl-and-Chimayo-wool Sweetwater Ranch club chair. Softening touches are added by Elizabeth Eakins's handmade rug and Diane Cole Ross's graceful rustic rocker.*
Photo © 2000 David Swift.

*A fire screen by metalworker Glenn Gilmore is refined enough for sophisticated settings, yet speaks to the wilderness at the same time.* Photo courtesy of the artist.

"Today," says Marty Kruzich of Martin-Harris Gallery in Jackson Hole, "we're seeing all kinds of western homes and a mixture of furnishing styles. People will bring their furniture from home—just like in the old days when they put their piano on the back of their Conestoga wagon." Bob Brown, longtime owner of the Big Horn Gallery in Cody, Wyoming, sees complete handcrafted environments as well as individually showcased one-of-a-kind pieces. "People who move here from back East or the Midwest are very excited about being in the West and generally have log homes up in the mountains. They'll often decorate with a very western look, sometimes with a whole suite of furniture from a particular shop. Then another homeowner might have just one handmade chair as a decorative element. They'll treat the piece as art. It's like that with saddles. About half the people who buy them in a gallery put them on a horse. The other half," he notes, "put them in the living room."

In the typical cowboy-chic living room, over-stuffed couches and deep Molesworth-inspired club chairs invite lounging while oversized upholstered ottomans offer a variation on the traditional coffee table, providing softer edges, a more casual feeling, and extra seating. Curtains may be passed over in favor of unimpeded views, or made of draping, luxuriant leather (handmade and often trimmed with beadwork) to offset sometimes-unforgiving interior log walls. A room might follow a unified western theme, carried through from chandeliers to chair backs. Increasingly, though, interiors showcase a mix of influences, reflecting the owners' passions or interests, whether for American primitive antiques, southwestern pottery, vintage Yellowstone souvenirs, or antique hand-carved doors from India.

*When used architecturally, found pieces of crooked wood add warmth and character to a living room in Big Sky, Montana. Says Merle Adams of Big Timber Works in Gallatin Gateway, Montana, "We make our buildings a representation of where we live. The design is simple, but the work and materials take it out of the ordinary." The furnishings are by New West.* Photo © 2000 Lynn Donaldson.

*Wild West Designs made the fireplace screen and massive chandeliers for this Girl Scout camp, Camp Cloud Rim, near Park City, Utah. The furniture invites sprawling, and the canoe speaks to prototypical camp activities.* Photo © Alan Blakely.

*Architect Kirk Michels designed this stone-and-timber great room in a house on a working ranch in Montana, which incorporates timbers from the rail bed near the Great Salt Lake and stone from the owner's native Texas. Stickley chairs and Mission-style lamps are paired with a table made locally from an ox yoke.* Photo © 2000 Lynn Donaldson.

[ 57 ]

*New York designer Will Hooper likes ottomans—here covered in an 1870s Scottish paisley shawl, with a tray made by a local craftsman on top—in place of coffee tables in contemporary western homes. "You can put drinks on it, fruit in a bowl, pistachios. You can put your feet up and look at the view. Hopefully it's pretty, but it's supposed to be convivial."*
Photo © 2000 Lynn Donaldson.

The challenges inherent in grand western spaces include balancing the sweeping vistas out the window with the interior space, making soaring rooms cozy, and adding warmth and texture to the typical exposed wood and stone surfaces. Massive couches, a low ottoman, and a richly textured rug do the job here. The couches, designed by Will Hooper and made by New West, having a vaguely art deco feel in their curved arms, have been westernized with applied pole. Linen burlap curtains add a touch of elegance while providing textile relief from the exposed wood. Photo © 2000 Lynn Donaldson.

In a Wild West Designs roomscape, one is drawn to the lighting. The chandeliers—with scenes of elk grazing in a lodgepole forest, or mounted Indians chasing buffalo around a tepee—incorporate three-dimensional figures of cast bronze. Light emanating from within reflects off the figures' rounded surfaces and up into the details above: branches of the trees, for instance, or the interior of a tepee. At night, the fireplace draws the eye, perhaps with a mountainscape made into a fire screen. The flickering of flames lends vigor to a mountainscape and creates movement in wildlife or cowboy figures.

These functional sculptures designed by Utah artist Peter Fillerup have become favorites of designers and homeowners looking for the warmth that bronze conveys. A line of furniture includes leather couches with inset bronze panels, willow chairs incorporating beadwork, and cast-bronze drawer pulls and handles. More recent interior commissions have ranged far afield to include leaded-glass windows, inlaid wood floors, and ceramic tiles.

Cast-bronze work is Fillerup's signature. He begins with charcoal and paper, passing through the sculpting stages to the final step of pouring molten bronze into molds. The work is cast in his own foundry. Certain parts are standard, but every piece is custom made. "It's a long process," Fillerup says.

Fillerup grew up in an artistic household, but the turning point came when as a young man working the oil fields in Utah he met up with his father in Oklahoma for a Cowboy Artists of America show. "On the way back I was sitting next to artist Harry Jackson and I thought, 'Gosh, if Harry can do it, I can do it.'"

While a college student, Fillerup got a chance to work for the internationally acclaimed sculptor Avard Fairbanks. "I was twenty-one years old. He paid me $50 a week and it was the greatest experience of my life. I did everything from vacuuming the floor to doing armatures for fifteen-foot statues. I went to Italy with him. By the end of the three years, he would do half a bust and say, 'You do the other half.'"

Fillerup received his first commission while working for Fairbanks—a fountain piece for a public space in Salt Lake City—and by the late 1970s had set up his own studio. In 1990 he was approached by craftsman Jim Covert to fashion some cast-bronze pieces for a desk. One of their first collaborations now resides in the permanent collection of the Buffalo Bill Historical Center.

A unique western aesthetic defines Fillerup's work. "Being from Cody and having grown up in the West, my work is firmly in the western school. I grew up on the North Fork of the Shoshone River in an old ranch house. It was a good-sized house and had an elegant feel to it. That house had quite an impact on my understanding of western art. Dad's law office was filled with Molesworth furniture, and my dining room table came into the Bighorn Basin in a wagon."

Fillerup strives for stylistic and historic accuracy—using the same type of beads from the original trade source in England as the Plains Indians would have used, for instance. His art has achieved its goal, he says, if it "throws you back to that time period, either consciously or subconsciously."

"I was twenty-one years old. He paid me $50 a week and it was the greatest experience of my life. I did everything from vacuuming the floor to doing armatures for fifteen-foot statues. I went to Italy with him. By the end of the three years, he would do half a bust and say, 'You do the other half.'"

*One open room combines living room, dining room, kitchen, and game room with mounted heads on the wall and a billiard table at the far end. A chandelier by Peter Fillerup lights a blue-leather card table and keyhole chairs from New West, a table out of Mexico made from an old door with legs from ox yokes, and an "art chair" by Mike Patrick of New West. The stone-top cabinet in the background was designed by the homeowner and features a tooled leather front and cow-hoof feet.* Photo © 2000 David Fitzgerald & Associates.

*Classic western imagery—in this case a stagecoach scene designed by artist Bill Schenck—feels right at home in a southwestern setting.* Photo © Jack Kotz.

James Howard made this intricate twig-and-snowshoe table from his home in Long Lake, New York. The primitive painting of a mountain lion stalking a deer was painted by Andrew Jackson, a Dutch immigrant to Montana, in Kalispell around the turn of the century. Photo © 2000 Lynn Donaldson.

*A stunning bookcase by Montana craftswoman Diane Cole Ross runs the width of a library in a house filled with books relevant to the region's culture and history. The warmth of its painted finish with chip-carved details was achieved by applying several coats of stain. Cole Ross then sanded it, applied other colors, sanded again, and applied a sienna glaze. The bookcase serves as the "touchstone" of the home, which is punctuated by period lighting fixtures such as the turn-of-the-century amber art-glass bell fixture with hammered brass canopy.* Photo © 2000 Lynn Donaldson.

A close look at the inlay detail reveals the intricacy of Mike Elliott's craftsmanship. "My inspiration comes from nature," says this seasoned ranch hand. Photo © Jeff Hinds.

The door panels and cabinets of this solid-pine armoire covered with Nevada barn wood feature 1,400 willow and wild-rose twigs laid side by side to create a one-inch border. California artisan Mike Elliott cut and inlaid 912 triangles of naturally colored plantation-grown hardwoods for the inside border, and finished it with a crown piece and footing of old fence rails and handles made from ponderosa pine. Photo © Jeff Hinds.

A suite of living room furniture combines an unusual cherry coffee table with juniper legs and a shelf of iron bars by Jim Covert, a heavy burl armchair from Sweetwater Ranch, and an original Thomas Molesworth end table. The fire screen borrows a mountains-and-sun motif from a 1930s Molesworth chair. The rug by New York designer Elizabeth Eakins is a play on the homeowner's collection of Nez Perce beaded bags, with the leaf motif taken from a beaded tobacco pouch and a border reminiscent of horsehair rope.
Photo © 2000 David Swift.

In this basswood fireplace mantel by Sun Valley artist Jack Burgess, a highly detailed carved bighorn ram's head is flanked by a swimming trout and sockeye salmon against a simple backdrop. Photo © Kevin Syms Photography.

*Brian Goff commissioned three distinctive willow pieces from Michigan craftsman Clifton Monteith for this home. A birch-bark canoe lends a hint of the Adirondacks to the western theme set by a sculpted fire screen by Peter Fillerup, a coffee table by Roy Fisk, and Native American pottery.* Photo © 2000 David Swift.

One of the best-known crafts-men in the West, Mike Patrick came across his trade by accident. This fourth-generation Cody cattle rancher had absorbed the influence of Thomas Molesworth by osmosis, having partly grown up in his grandfather's Molesworth-decorated ranch house. A builder of log homes and cabinetry, it wasn't until he disassembled an eighty-year-old windbreak in the late 1980s that he felt compelled to make a piece of furniture. The weathered slats had achieved a texture and character over the years that cried out, Patrick thought, to be preserved and reused, in this case as a desk.

One piece led to the next, and with a few designs under his belt and a handful of commissions from friends and neighbors in the Cody area, Patrick quit his job and launched, with his wife, Virginia, the effort that would grow to become New West. At first, he recalls, "It was my take on western. The designs were fairly traditional—dry sinks and hutches with antler pulls, for instance. I just put together this little collection."

In 1988, the Patricks sent their first catalog to a friend in New York, and that resulted in one piece being featured in the *New York Times*. After that, New West was off and running. While signa-ture New West pieces draw on the Molesworth style—with lots of applied pole, heavy burl, fringed and colored leather, rawhide lampshades, and keyhole dining chairs—Patrick uses it merely as a starting point. "I don't do reproductions; I do interpretations," he says. "And my designs still react against kitchiness. I want to make the designs cleaner."

Arts & Crafts and art deco, for instance, are two stylistic movements that find expression in his work. And New West's "anti-gravity table," now part of the permanent collection of the Buffalo Bill Historical Center through the 1998 Switchback Ranch Purchase Award, defies categorization. An unusual pine burl slab extends from atop a beautifully curved and striated juniper pedestal; the top is balanced from one end, making the piece appear to float in the air.

Patrick founded the Western Design Conference in 1993, and through supporting other craftsmen was instrumental in creating an industry. Working with fellow craftsmen in Cody, Patrick said, "We had to get a vocabulary going that people understood. Most of the western work was post-and-pole being done out of garages in Vail. No one had seen how sophisticated western could be." The Western Design Conference changed that by bringing together some of the top

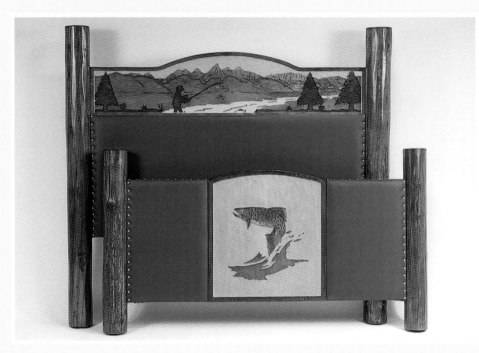

Photo: Ron Maier.

*Mike and Virginia Patrick's living room is a showcase for New West's Molesworth-inspired furniture and for Cody artists such as Stephan Halvorsen.* Photo © Ron Maier.

designers working in the style, simultaneously introducing them to each other and to the public. "The Western Design Conference has really driven creativity and quality. You know you better show up with your guns loaded. You think you've done the best thing, and then you see what else is there and you're humbled."

Seeing the work of other craftspeople, working closely with clients, and drawing on the talents of his own hand-picked team are the things that invigorate Patrick's designs. "Probably the thing I do best is gather good people around me and make use of their talents," says Patrick, whose company now employs a dozen people and provides regular work to about ten contract artisans, from metalworkers and bead workers to fine artists. "It's fun to sit down with the old portfolios and see how far you've come," he reflects. "For one thing you see an improvement in quality, but you also see an evolution in design, both in vocabulary and expression."

*Pueblo style, art deco, and Thomas Molesworth meet in artist Bill Schenck's Santa Fe home. His collaborations with craftsman Steve Alvorsen "go way beyond what Molesworth ever did."* Photo courtesy of the artist.

*Fourth-generation Idahoan R. Dana Merrill fashions furniture, as in this functional armoire, that hearkens back to the pioneer days. He uses reclaimed barn wood for its rich, warm patina and found objects such as leather, tobacco cans, Coke™ openers, and horse-harness rings. Each of Merrill's pieces bears a whimsical identification: wire threaded through small holes on either side of a natural fissure in the wood, and "stitched" across the crack.* Photo © Jack Kotz.

*A birch-bark wet bar built by Diane Cole Ross and designed in conjunction with Van Bryan of Apogee Architects in Bozeman, Montana, is the focal point of this ranch living room. "This is the first piece we designed, and it was really rewarding," recalls Bryan. "Not only is it functional, it's aesthetic and fits the character of the room. It serves the purpose very well without appearing as an afterthought."* Photo © 2000 Lynn Donaldson.

[ 71 ]

*MKR Design's custom-made rugs are hand tufted and colored
to fit any décor—or breed of dog.* Photo courtesy of the artist.

*A century-old cabin offers a cozy retreat for guests at UXU
Ranch in Wyoming, whose brand appears throughout on
furniture created by New West.* Photo © 2000 Dewey Vanderhoff.

[ 72 ]

Master woodworker John Bryan spends hundreds of hours on his carved pieces, such as this angling-themed fireplace surround from his Streamside Series. Although he studied furniture design at the University of New Hampshire, during which time he won an international student design competition, he is self-taught as a carver. Bryan, who works alone, tries not to look at other peoples' work; he takes his inspiration from nature and from the lives of his clients. "I want to hold on to whatever innocence and originality I have and apply it to whatever opportunities come my way," he says. He refers to his twenty-three-year experience as a craftsman as a "journey" and admits, "I could probably write a short novel on all the years people weren't knocking on my door. There's no shortcut on the dues you have to pay. But it's probably the most satisfying way to spend your life." Both photos © Warren Roos.

*Jackson Hole sculptor John Mortensen's Rainbow Trail Collection is a combination of cast-bronze sculpture, wood, and stone. Each piece includes designs that are shaped, molded, then cast at the foundry. Says Mortensen, "This gives each work a sculpted depth, a true bas-relief, and offers a variety of patinas." The "Indian and Buffalo" chandelier was one of several similar chandeliers created for a house in Wyoming's Wind River Mountains. Forty-eight inches in diameter with mica across the bottom, it features a buffalo hunt.* Photo courtesy of the artist.

# CHRIS CHAPMAN, CHAPMAN DESIGN

Chris Chapman brings a unique background to her leatherwork furniture. In her previous life she developed her interest in historical clothing into an expertise in historically accurate re-creations. From quillwork to beadwork, pre–Revolutionary War clothing and fur-trader outfits to shooting pouches, Chapman studied as many pieces as she could get her hands on and read voraciously. Then in 1987 she moved to the top of a mesa near Aspen. "As soon as I moved to Colorado, I was able to sell the work I had been doing. It just hadn't been appreciated in the same way in the Midwest."

In 1991, she made the first of the leather-wrapped pieces that are now her life's work. Although she wasn't the first to apply leather to wooden frames, she says, "Everything else I'd seen had been poorly done, because the maker's only reference had been saddle making. They are limited by that. I didn't come from a saddle-making background. I had been doing leatherwork for thirty years. My historical research and reproduction work went all the way back to sixteenth-century Europe. I had seen so many different styles and ways of putting things together in museums and private collections that when I started making furniture, everything came together."

The results are masterworks—from enormous armoires to mirrors and custom cabinetry—that have a warm, comforting presence, the texture of a well-worn saddle, and a patina of age and loving use. Close inspection reveals intricate surface tooling, decoration, and shading that bring out the form of the piece as well as the designs worked into the leather.

"The high-relief technique I've invented is like sculpting from underneath. It's similar to repoussé metalwork. Sometimes it's layers of leather, literally carved and sculpted and shaped, then overlaid with another piece of leather, which is worked to pull out the detail."

Her Best of Show award winner in the 1998 Western Design Conference

was a king-sized bed bearing hand-forged iron crosses at the center of the head- and footboards. For this piece, she developed a decorative border trim that simulated Spanish chip carving in a raised pattern. The following year's entry was an armoire whose upper door panels featured a scene with mule deer, elk, buffalo, and sandhill cranes set amidst sage and ponderosa pines against the Teton Mountains.

For Chapman, art has proved both an outlet for creativity and a way of finding inner peace. Now that she has the luxury of picking and choosing her clients and jobs, the goal is to find a balance between work and life. She has been doing a lot of installations, such as built-in bars and leather-wrapped barrel-vaulted ceilings for a house in Texas. But she doesn't want to do the production-type work anymore. She likes to work with people and have relationships with her clients.

"I try to build things that will be just as appealing a hundred years from now. The kind of person who buys my things isn't buying because it's a trend, but because they want this piece for their grandchildren."

*A massive armoire showcases Chris Chapman's unique technique with leather sculpting, in which leather is worked into a pattern underneath the surface. Both photos: David O. Marlow.*

*Designer Annette Stelmack of Associates III in Denver combined just a touch of western—in the antler-encircled leather footstool—with comfortable overstuffed couches and chairs, a Tiffany lamp, upholstered hickory chairs, and mountain views.*
Photo: David O. Marlow.

*Craftsman Lester Santos's signature is his use of organically shaped pieces of wood and hand-painted images inspired by Native American ledger paintings.* Photo © 2000 J. K. Lawrence.

Van Bryan of Apogee Architects reworked an existing ranch building in Montana that was "very unsympathetic, it had no sense of intimacy" by adding beam work and soffits to "bring everything down to a human scale." Local river rock, a hair-on-cowhide ottoman, antler lighting fixtures, and Indian-drum end tables anchor the room in the American West. "All through the house we'd talked about comfort and durability. There's a real sense of permanence inherent in the logs. A lot of the houses we do go far beyond trying to create a particular image. Our clients are here to relax and to enjoy the Montana experience, not to put on airs." Photo © 2000 Lynn Donaldson.

A cut-metal lodgepole forest grows through a
sandstone tabletop in the work of Pat Olson.
Photo courtesy of the artist.

# Convivial Places

### KITCHENS AND DINING ROOMS

One of the many icons of the Old West is the chuckwagon, from which hearty meals were dished out to hungry cowhands who'd rustled up an honest appetite after trailing cattle all day. It's an undisputed fact that food tastes better when served outdoors, so the most successful indoor cooking and eating spaces should combine function with a taste of the natural surroundings.

To achieve the latter, there may be windows open to the view, regional artwork substituted for additional windows, furniture and fixtures made from natural materials (antlers, for instance), or historic artifacts such as wagon wheels or old doors worked into the design scheme. For example, a sideboard created by fourth-generation Idahoan Dana Merrill, made entirely from reclaimed materials found in old barns (even down to the drawer pulls made from horse harnesses), adds textural and historical richness to any space. Bar stools by Colorado artisan Greg Race speak to Colorado's history in its form yet meets the present in contemporary use and interpretation of traditional materials. For these artists, function is a given;

they expect their work to stand up to tough treatment and to last longer than a lifetime.

In keeping with the character of Big Sky Country, dining areas generally open up to the rest of the living area, and the kitchen opens to both. The dining area might be elevated or sunken and the kitchen delineated by a countertop to subconsciously set these areas apart from the other spaces. From a practical viewpoint, such a layout provides easier circulation and promotes more-efficient use of all the space. The result fosters a feeling of conviviality.

The dining room's focal point may be the lighting fixture above the table. The fixture can help bring the ceiling down visually to create a more intimate space. The spotlighting of the table generates a warm glow that draws together the people within its reach, much like a campfire. A classic antler chandelier can produce a variety of effects, depending on the type and configuration of the antlers. Wide, heavy moose antlers add visual weight and serve to anchor the scene, while

*A fabulous sculpted bronze chandelier by Utah artist Peter Fillerup surmounts a dining table and chairs by Sweetwater Ranch against a backdrop created by an antique Navajo rug in a home just south of Grand Teton National Park.* Photo © 2000 David Swift.

[82]

*Custom concrete countertops, cabinets made to look reclaimed, lighting fixtures with parchment-and-barbed-wire shades, and tiles incorporating images of moose, bear, deer, antelope, and other native wildlife combine in a space that's as unconfined as the great outdoors.*
Photo © 2000 Lynn Donaldson.

elk antlers seem to float, creating an almost lacy effect with their spaced tines. The result is a grace note that can lighten a more formal dining area, such as one with a massive rectangular wooden table lined with stately rows of upholstered chairs.

In contrast, a round table with a built-in lazy Susan made by a master craftsman lends informality to a house built for a woman with a background in design. The dining area, which opens to the kitchen, fosters a deliberate simplicity; its unadorned windows, plain wooden floors, southwestern-striped upholstery on Old Hickory–style chairs, and graceful antler chandelier showcase the craftsmanship of the table; its base is a copper-banded pedestal, and the applied half-pole apron under the tabletop is echoed under the lazy

Susan. The homeowner collaborated with the craftsman on all the custom-made furnishings in her snow-country home. "We talked about everything before we did it," she notes. "I really believe in what these craftsmen are doing. They're not derivative; they're truly creative."

For some, preparing food is as fulfilling as eating it. Western kitchens are getting their due in handcrafted cabinetry, often distressed or painted to evoke a feeling of age. Countertops range from butcher block to granite to poured concrete, often with insets or backsplashes of handcrafted tiles or remnants of stone bearing fossil imprints. Wood, stone, tile, or practical high-tech linoleum substitutes are classic western kitchen elements.

Nowhere is an open floor plan more relevant and practical than in the kitchen, where it goes hand in hand with a casual approach to living and encourages family and guests to congregate. In a home designed by Van Bryan of Apogee Architects, "the kitchen was meant to be a real focal point. This couple spends a lot of time entertaining, and the woman loves to cook. Everyone always seems to end up in the kitchen and you get a lot of people milling around, enjoying what's taking place." Thus, custom concrete countertops, cabinets made to look reclaimed, lighting fixtures with parchment-and-barbed-wire shades, and tiles

*An elk-antler chandelier by Mike Wilson, of Jackson Hole, floats above a table with a copper-banded pedestal base and applied half-pole aprons designed by the homeowner in conjunction with artisan Jim Covert. The unique lazy Susan pedestal was designed for practical living in a home frequently filled with grandchildren. The upholstered hickory chairs are from Indiana.*
Photo © 2000 David Swift.

incorporating images of native wildlife combine in a space that's as unconfined as the great outdoors.

A leisurely meal around the dining table affords an opportunity for appreciating handcrafted details. The chairs and table—whether wood (rough-textured or hand-sanded to silkiness), smooth leather, or rough stone—provide a tactile experience, while close-up views of lighting fixtures, candleholders, and a hutch or corner piece displaying pottery or other treasures offer a chance to appreciate the details of quality workmanship.

In the Mountain West, the vistas outside can be as intriguing as the art on the walls. In a Montana home furnished by New York designer Will Hooper, the dining room is a simple space with a handcrafted trestle table commissioned locally, a practical pass-through to the kitchen, one superlative painting, and plenty of windows, all unadorned.

"What was superior about the client," Hooper reflects, "was that everything had to have a function. He loves the land and the history. He's the first person up in the morning, going out to work with the animals. He wanted something real and he wanted to bring the land in as much as possible. The wood of the outdoors is in the house. The way you look at the view outside

*Martha Cielesz's contemporary western vernacular combines the funky with the whimsical in this unique cabinet with deer-leg pulls. It is situated over a small dining table adorned with collectibles.* Photo courtesy of the artist.

is the same as you see it from the house. I didn't want to keep him from it."

The spaces in which we prepare and eat our meals may be a far cry from the chuckwagon, but the end result—honest food in a distinctive setting—should be the same.

*In a Montana home furnished by New York designer Will Hooper, the dining room is a simple space with a handcrafted trestle table by Davis-Torres in Bozeman, Montana, and chairs from New West. A practical pass-through to the kitchen is lined with counter stools from the Old Hickory Company, one superlative painting, and plenty of unadorned windows. A turn-of-the-century Persian carpet and Arts & Crafts–style wainscoting create an enveloping warmth.* Photo © 2000 Lynn Donaldson.

*Upholstered chairs by Wyoming furniture maker Lester Santos add required elegance to a dining area crowned by a dramatic oil painting by Albert Bierstadt.* Photo © 2000 Elijah Cobb.

In a home showcasing the work of artisans Ron and Jean Shanor, even the windows are surmounted by treatments fashioned from tiny burls. A large armoire of lodgepole pine burl logs and trimmed with contrasting flat pieces of aged Douglas fir is accented with polished antler handles and drawer pulls. Photo © 2000 Elijah Cobb.

Rob Mazza has been influenced by many different styles in his thirteen years as a furniture maker. Being from New England, the simple elegance of Shaker design had always appealed to him. Later, introduced to the Arts & Crafts movement by an architect friend, he was drawn to the work of architect/designers Charles and Henry Greene. In both cases, his interest came too early to capitalize on the later explosion of popular demand for those styles.

Mazza is self-taught through books and hands-on training as a carpenter. "My grandfather was a carpenter and he influenced me somewhat. My mom was in the arts and had some art training; my dad was a real practical guy, and the two came together in me. I spent three weeks in college and said, 'Forget it; I'm going to the college of the world.'"

After landing in Montana in 1975, he "just ended up staying. Summer became fall and fall become winter. There were a bunch of us working as carpenters, partying, and spending time in nature." Eventually his foremen noticed that he "was more visionary and detail oriented. I would always be the one assigned to build the curved staircase," he says. Living in the Gallatin River canyon near the northwest corner of Yellowstone National Park, he noticed the old dude-ranch furniture that was around on porches and out in the weather not attracting much notice and certainly not any special care. "I saw all that homemade furniture," he recalls, "and I think I mentally said, 'I'm going to make this stuff one day.'"

He started making furniture part-time, and over a period of years the work became full-time. Although he initially made a name for himself working in the style of Thomas Molesworth, today his work encompasses many styles and influences and is no longer so readily identifiable as "cowboy." His work has

Photo courtesy of the artist.

evolved right along with the definition of *western.*

"I've gotten away from the cowboy look and the Molesworth influence. I'm pretty restrained. And I've never totally gotten away from my New England roots." Thus, a commission for a set of eight dining room chairs of lodgepole pine combines spindles of diamond willow with a rush-weave seat. "Most of my work is pretty delicate as far as lodgepole is concerned."

While working on a commission for the lobby furniture of a Bozeman inn, he got his chance to combine Arts & Crafts with western. "It's kind of a darker Arts & Crafts look with fir, lodgepole, black leather, and wrought iron."

He's open to influences that will keep his work fresh. "I'm trying to be creative," he says. A newer piece is a free-form bench combining curvy structural pieces of lodgepole pine with copper banding. In 1997, Mazza and his wife spent five months in Kenya and Uganda as missionaries, followed by a vacation in Scotland. A follow-up work combines a stone top with primitive Arts & Crafts forms. "Must be the influence of all those castles in Scotland," he laughs.

Africa, of course, left its mark as well. "When I returned from Africa, I did a piece with yellow-headed blackbirds that we see around here. I produced this piece with carved, brightly painted blackbirds. It looks like Africa meets Montana meets Kontiki. It still hasn't sold."

Which is okay, he insists. "I think people ought to push the boundaries a little."

*A table with an applied-pole apron by Jim Boot and diamondback willow chairs by Rob Mazza—both Montana craftsmen—looks out on the nearby mountains in Big Sky, Montana. The signed oil painting circa 1945 of a cowboy observing grazing bison is by Bernard Hoffman, one of a pair to come out of Frontier Town, a tourist resort near Helena. The double antler chandelier is by New West.* Photo © 2000 Lynn Donaldson.

*Poured concrete countertops designed by Kirk Michels and Reid Erickson lend surprising warmth and texture to this well-laid-out kitchen.* Photo © 2000 Lynn Donaldson.

*Dining is the primary indoor activity at the Girl Scouts' Camp Cloud Rim near Park City, Utah. A huge great room is lit by custom-made chandeliers by Utah artist Peter Fillerup, who also made the fire screen.* Photo © Alan Blakely.

With its unusual combination and treatment of materials and its distinctive designs, Quandary Design is turning heads. In addition to attracting the attention of well-known interior designers, the company won the 1997 Western Design Conference's Switchback Ranch Purchase Award in its first year of participation (and its first year of business).

"What we're trying to do," explains Greg Race, "is blend some of the traditional forms and shapes, like the stylized cabriolet Queen Anne–style legs, and take the guts and meat of it but distill it down to something really simple, really traditional. That's what I'm trying to do with most of my work. We're after a look that's western but contemporary."

Quandary Design's "The Stray Horse Sideboard" has doors of patinated copper, a distressed saddle-leather-covered base, steel legs and doorframes, and leather-covered shelves. The base of a glass-topped dining table is of steel, copper, and leather, with matching chairs upholstered in rich, deep-red leather. The work is decidedly cowboy chic: at home in the western setting, but with a distinct contemporary edge.

"All my work is empirically based," Race continues. "I don't have any formal training. I'm not super-analytical. When I get interested in something, I research a lot. My brother is an art historian, and he helps me place things in historical context. But other than shop class in grammar school, I'd never really been in a wood shop. It's mostly just trial and error. I just keep messing things up, then taking the neat effects and using them over again. I'll start raw and not worry about doing things really accurately at first, then I narrow in based on a theory or concept."

A New England native, Race has a quiet intensity that served him well in his first career as a top-ranked snowboarder and product tester. It upheld him through the sacrifices one makes in an attempt to make ends meet in the Rocky Mountain high country. ("I slept in a borrowed van for five months while saving up enough money to start this furniture business.") Now he brings it to bear on his furniture designs, which bring as much complexity as is possible to conservative forms with a western look.

> "A lot of what I'm doing is kind of backwards from what other western furniture makers are doing, where the materials and raw forms determine the shape of the pieces. I want to take the materials and put them into a contrived form, a disciplined structure, but make them look natural."

Says the craftsman: "A lot of what I'm doing is kind of backwards from what other western furniture makers are doing, where the materials and raw forms determine the shape of the pieces. I want to take the materials and put them into a contrived form, a disciplined structure, but make them look natural."

And that's not necessarily at odds with the western-design aesthetic. "Everything man-made is a fabrication. Everything we touch is natural until we touch it; then it's man-made. I don't have a hang-up about using man-made or contrived materials as long as visually the piece has some interest and complexity. I love trying to work through an idea. That's far more worthwhile than the cash. It gives me a place to do something fairly conservative in design, but almost limitless within that boundary. What interests me is furniture that stands on its own within an interior space. Every piece should be able to stand by itself, should be well-designed and thoughtful, and should carry its own weight."

*Bar stools crafted by Greg Race of Quandary Design in Colorado would be a classy addition to a home kitchen. Here, they complement an unusual western bar at The Buffalo Bar & Grill inside the newly constructed Yellowstone Club near Big Sky, Montana. The bar, by New Creation Cabinetry, features embossed tin on recycled barn wood with ornamental carving; highlights have been airbrushed onto the tin and wood.* Photo © Rob Wilke.

Chris Chapman's unique style of leather work turned an ordinary kitchen bar with stools into an extraordinary room divider. It wouldn't surprise a working cowboy to learn that leather can stand up to the rigors of daily meal service, including the spills and wipe-ups. Photo: David O. Marlow.

A massive carved dining table by New Creation Cabinetry is flanked by large cowhide-covered wing chairs and lit by a moose-antler chandelier. The table makes the most of an expansive view of Lone Mountain from the Yellowstone Club near Big Sky, Montana. Photo © Rob Wilke.

Reidar Wahl's furniture is the product of two cultures and an array of influences. A native of Norway, Wahl came to the United States at age twenty-one as a professional ski racer and lived in Telluride, Colorado, for twelve years before moving to northern Idaho.

In Norway, he grew up with Scandinavian antiques and the refined country-folk furniture the region is renowned for. In southern Colorado, he was exposed to centuries-old southwestern traditions of craftsmanship in furniture and folk art, as well as a mix of the best in contemporary western furnishings and fine art. In Idaho, Wahl settled in a region heavily populated by descendants of pioneers who emigrated from Scandinavia.

Wahl's furniture, like his life, has come full circle, a comfortable blend of Norwegian, southwestern, and western influences equally at home in an adobe in New Mexico, a stave-constructed wooden building in Norway, or a log cabin in the Rockies. A sturdy trestle table, for instance, is made from two thick pine planks still bearing the marks of the circular saw used to cut them, held together with butterfly inlays and mortise-and-through-tenon joinery. The piece, while decidedly rustic-western, is actually a near-replica of tables Wahl has seen "by the hundreds" in Norway. The door of a ponderosa-pine armoire bears vertical diamond cutouts that speak both to cutouts found in furniture throughout the Southwest and to those frequently employed as a decorative and functional motif in Scandinavian doors and log construction.

A sturdily built mortise-and-through-tenon bench based on photos of a 300-year-old New Mexican piece is made western through its upholstery, with decorative chip carving adding interest on the vertical planes.

Wahl gave up professional skiing to become a craftsman in 1988 while he was sidelined by a knee operation; he had been contemplating a career in clothing design when his wife suggested he build some furniture for their apartment. "I went to Wal-Mart and bought a drill and a jig saw and a little circular saw, and after that I went to the hardware store and bought some lumber. At the time," he reflects, "I was pretty ignorant."

He found he had a passion for furniture. On trips to Norway he'd indulge his interest in the history of furniture by visiting the Norwegian Folk Art Museum in Oslo, where his uncle was longtime curator. It is "one of the most interesting museums in the world," he says, "filled with antique furniture and old buildings, from a stave church to a full farmhouse settlement with barns. I could take out my notepad and go nuts. I would get down on my hands and knees and see how things were put together." Meanwhile, he was educating himself by reading voraciously about furniture making. After more than a decade of study, he says, "I know how to put a piece of furniture together. Now my job is to be creative and to make beautiful things.

"I use only mortise-and-through-tenon joinery, and try to use as little plywood as possible because even though it's strong it's not authentic," Wahl explains. "Dimensions are incredibly important: I won't build a piece of furniture with three-quarter-inch doors; they have to be an inch, or an inch and a half. There are a lot of things you can't do on

machines that you can do by hand. On a ladder-back chair, I might do the whole back by hand to get that feeling of how it was done in the old days. I'm not into skimping on style and function. I like simple things that give a joyful feeling. And I want my furniture to be around for a long time."

*A cheerful kitchen in Telluride was designed, built, and furnished by Norwegian craftsman Reidar Wahl. It showcases his unique blend of southwestern, Scandinavian, and western influences.* Both photos courtesy of the artist.

"You don't want to get too nostalgic," says R. Dana Merrill, "but western design was born of need. I try to build things people need."

Merrill's designs hearken back to the days when a homesteader's big annual expenditure might be sending off to Sears & Roebuck for a pie safe or Hoosier. Using warm, richly patinated weathered wood, Merrill's cabinets, sideboards, and desks feature glass-fronted compartments, woven-wire racks, cubbyholes, wing-like shelves, and hooks in unexpected places. He incorporates reclaimed barn wood, old horse harnesses, and found objects such as rusty nails, harness rings, bits, leather reins, tobacco cans, and scavenged wood.

"I'm a fourth-generation Idahoan," Merrill explains. "I spent a lot of my time on family ranches. That's where I draw most of my inspiration, really. Many of my grandfather's doors had leather hinges. Everything was put together with things that he found. For one thing, he was poor. But also, it was a long way to town; you couldn't get people to come out. They made a lot of their own tools. They even hand-forged some things. These people were very self-reliant, and self-reliance is a very important part of western thought. Even for the new westerners, people from the East come here looking for that romance. Reusing what you have and trying to make do is important; I catch myself doing it even when I don't have to. I try to portray that in my art and in the materials I use."

Merrill lives with his wife and son on an old homestead at the edge of the Frank Church Wilderness, just down the Salmon River from an old mining ghost town. "It is even more rural here than southern Idaho. Some of these ranchers live two hours from town," he points out. So no one questions his use of the old barn wood he's known to collect. In fact, he says, ranchers often pull up in his yard with a truck full of wood and old leather and ask if he could use the stuff.

Merrill uses only reclaimed wood. "I use fir and pine, mostly. That's what grows locally around here. It comes from neighboring ranches and my own. It's beautiful wood, baked for 100 years in the sun. I plane down all the old wood so it has integrity again, but there's still a patina that's baked through, and the old nail holes are still there.

"I try not to salvage it unless it's going to be burned anyway. I've harvested barns, miner's shacks, even chicken coops. A lot of my ideas for the appointments on my furniture come to me when I'm tearing down buildings; I find beautiful pieces of hardware lying around."

A full-time furniture maker since 1993, Merrill is also a fine artist and printmaker (he holds both a BFA and an MFA). His studies have exposed him to the work of such master designers as Arts & Crafts architects Greene & Greene, whose ideas are conveyed subtly in some of Merrill's pieces in the use of walnut tenons and pegs on pine furniture.

He has also been influenced by antiques he has collected, as well as his Swedish ancestry on his mother's side. "I noticed that the Swedes would put a little tiny drawer at the top of an armoire, for instance, and I've used that idea in several pieces. Swedes weren't so uptight about using clear vertical grain;

they allowed natural fissures to appear in the piece, and I liked that. About four years ago I did stitching across a crack, and everyone was drawn to it. I don't know exactly why. Since then, every piece has it."

Each of Merrill's pieces bears this whimsical signature: wire threaded through small drilled holes and "stitched" across a crack. "I'll find a crack that needs support, then I'll sew it just like you'd sew a piece of material. Sometimes it's functional and makes it stronger, but sometimes it's just decorative. It says a lot about ingenuity. It represents my whole philosophy."

*Dana Merrill's pieces speak to the pioneer heritage of the West through their forms and through the use of old wood and reclaimed hardware.* Both photos courtesy of the artist.

*A small drop-leaf table on natural birch legs by Lupine Arts is a practical addition to a narrow hallway or cozy kitchen.* Photo © Chris Autio.

*A remarkable inlaid tabletop by Montana craftsman John Omohundro rests atop a stump whose natural root configuration suggests a woman's legs crossed at the ankles.* Photo © Chris Thompson.

*Legendary Furniture's Greg Mitchell, in Fayetteville, Arkansas, uses traditional mortise-and-tenon joinery to craft each of his pieces. His materials are seasoned hardwood branches and solid-wood lumber from the Ozarks. This table combines a cherry top with red-oak legs and a maple base.* Photo courtesy of the artist.

*Diane and Indy Corson of Lupine Arts show their distinctive style in this hutch through its signature twig-treatment style.* Photo © Chris Autio.

Amber Jean, an artist and sculptor in Montana, carved and painted this matching kitchen table and china hutch with a fish-in-stream motif and applied-pole apron. Photo courtesy of the artist.

Handles made of sticks and the application of red willow twigs bring the outdoors into this cozy western kitchen with cabinetry designed and built by Lupine Arts. Photo © Visions Photography.

Contemporary western design reaches new heights of elegance in the work of Chris Chapman's leather-wrapped dining table for ten and Glenn Gilmore's custom-forged fire screen. Photo: David O. Marlow.

# Angles of Repose

## BEDROOMS

There is an interesting paradox about the bedroom. It is the most intimate and in some ways most personal space in the house. Although we spend the largest portion of each day here, most of the time we are oblivious to our surroundings. The bedroom is a highly functional space, yet its ambience is crucial for effective rest and rejuvenation—whether its occupants have spent the day branding cattle or wrangling houseguests down ski slopes.

The bed is undoubtedly the centerpiece of the room, reflecting the personalities of those who sleep in it. Whether made of log or willow or reclaimed barn wood, whether leather-upholstered, beaded, painted, or natural, the handcrafted bed reflects the soul of the craftsman while revealing the nature of its owners.

"Beds are very personal, very intimate," reflects Montana craftswoman Diane Cole-Ross. "Usually people have a lot of ideas about how they want their bed to be. To me, that's the best part, getting a sense of what they want and then adding to that. I've done birch beds, mosaic twig head- and footboards, lodgepole-pine beds, and really basic bent willow. I like working with willow because of the branches and twists and forks. A canopy of twigs can make you feel like you're sleeping in a little forest. Another bed I made is like a nest because it's branched and curved and arched. For a Crow Indian friend, I made a lodgepole bed with big burls. She's a big, voluptuous woman, and the bed is big and curvy and round, and it fits her. For her, the bed is her lodge, her stability, her strength."

For one Wyoming couple, a massive, almost Gothic bed of fantastically twisted and forked juniper collected from the hills of the ranch constitutes the centerpiece of the room. Reaching high overhead, the bed is inset with a cast-bronze medallion of an Indian. The bed is practical—ample enough for the two children who clamber in after scary dreams, its posts sturdy enough to endure their daytime gymnastics sessions. Beyond leather curtains with hand-beaded panels lies a sliding-glass door to a deck, which extends into the leafy cottonwoods

*Everything is oversized in this stone room so it can hold its own with the grand Colorado scenery outside. Chris Chapman's massive leather-wrapped bed anchors the room.* Photo: David O. Marlow.

*From dead-standing trees he found on the ranch, Jim Covert built a massive, almost Gothic, juniper bed with fantastically twisted and forked wood reaching high overhead. The headboard is inset with a cast-bronze medallion of an Indian. Beyond the hand-beaded leather curtains by Lynda Covert lies a sliding-glass door to a deck, which juts out toward a cottonwood-lined creek. In the dressing room is a vanity designed for the homeowner by New West.* Photo © 2000 Elijah Cobb.

*Framed prints of Native Americans by Montana photographer L.A. Huffman lend a serene dignity to a neutrally colored guest bedroom. The large-scale bed with exposed knotholes is nestled among vintage wicker side tables and a New West leather-and-brass chest. Antique kerosene parlor lamps and a fancy paisley shawl circa 1875 add period accents.* Photo © 2000 Lynn Donaldson.

lining a creek that provides a relaxing serenade. Even on winter nights, nature runs right through the room in the form of a waterfall that cascades over rough-textured volcanic rocks collected from the immediate hillsides. The water flows into a hand-built bathtub that overlooks a spectacular valley defined by wildly shaped volcanic outcrops—"hoodoos" in local parlance. The drama of nature is the reference point.

In another ranch home, a guest room is simple and soothing. An oversized paneled bed, locally built to the designer's specifications and set against neutral floors and walls, creates a restful haven. The room speaks to the history of the region. A deft combination of contemporary furniture (a leather chest with the ranch brand in brass tacks) and period accents such as lamps and textiles from the last decades of the nineteenth century provide context for contemporary living.

Subtlety flies out the window when children are involved, and fun is the order of the day. A

little-girl's room in Wyoming combines a simple bent-log bed with a diminutive, leather-upholstered chaise lounge and a child-sized willow rocker. Red, both bold and playful, appears throughout the room in the bed linens, the leather top of a bedside table, and the leather appliqué and beadwork on pillows made by the child's godmother. A boy's room combines beaded curtains and a red leather hairy cowhide chair and ottoman with a computer and electric keyboard for an effect that is fun, western, boyish, and decidedly contemporary.

*Highlights of red add warmth and playfulness to a little-girl's room on a Wyoming cattle ranch. A simple log bed, a diminutive leather-upholstered chaise lounge festooned with hand-beaded pillows by Lynda Covert, a child's rocker of willow, a leather-topped side table by New West, and a hand-painted chest by northern California artist Rosemary Heon strike a balance between sophistication and fun.*
Photo © 2000 Elijah Cobb.

Increasingly, homeowners feel that the full expression of the western fantasy is best left to the kids' rooms. For other bedrooms, they might opt instead for an oversized floral-upholstered headboard against a backdrop of log walls and antler table lamps. A few handcrafted pieces—such as an organically curved bench with subtle carving details or a whimsical wall shelf and mirror with candleholders—stand out all the more against a neutral backdrop. Natural materials, with their unique shapes and variety of textures, combined

*A boy's room in Wyoming is fun, western, and decidedly boyish with its red leather and hairy cowhide chair and ottoman, designed by the boy at age five in conjunction with New West. The curtains are by Lynda Covert. A wagon-wheel light fixture and Plains Indian shields raise the visual interest to ceiling level. A child's rocker by Marshall Dominick holds a beaded pillow by Queen of the Plains. The computer and electric keyboard reveal a room both contemporary and lived-in.* Photo © 2000 Elijah Cobb.

*A whimsical shelf of juniper and leather with a mirror and rotating candlesticks combines Jim Covert's woodworking skills with the bead-working prowess of Lynda Covert. "It's a fantasy piece," says the homeowner.*
Photo © 2000 David Swift.

with a decided sense of comfort, are what define the contemporary western bedroom.

"A lot of people talk to me about the sense of peace or retreat that they want in their bedroom," says Diane Cole-Ross, "and I think natural materials help to create that feeling. The feeling that you want in your home is a metaphor, so I'm not surprised if people want a nest, or a smooth surface, or a rough surface with texture. I like to think it's not a trend, but a real need to surround ourselves with natural things. It used to be we weren't so removed from the natural world, but now we are, even here in Montana."

The ultimate western retreat conveys that sense of peace and enclosure as its handcrafted elements refer to the greater world beyond. These elements bring nature in while providing a refuge from its harshness.

*Cowboys, Indians, and nature are all represented in this bedroom designed by Brian Goff of Harker Design, who worked closely with Mike Livingston on the design of the dresser and matching mirror. Peter Fillerup's chair speaks to the culture of the Plains Indians while Diane Cole Ross's rustic bench gives "a different texture, more color, and a sense of permanence with the leather woven around the willow itself," says Goff.* Photo © 2000 David Swift.

*This bench by Lester Santos has a primitive feel, combining a traditional form with organically shaped accents and Santos's trademark hammering.* Photo © 2000 David Swift.

*Steve Alvorsen designed a dresser with pole supports and totemic elements from Northwest Coast tribes in an expanded west-ern vernacular. The piece is comfortable in artist Bill Schenck's Santa Fe home.* Photo © Jack Kotz.

*Jim Covert had never done "little girl" beds when he accepted this commission; he surprised the homeowner with the twins' initials carved into the footboards. On the wall hang beaded-leather crib quilts by Queen of the Plains.* Photo © Dewey Vanderhoff.

*The rooms at Camp Cloud Rim reflect the nature of the camp's activities in the classic hiker image on the chest of drawers by Wild West Designs.* Photo © 2000 Alan Blakely.

While studying range and soil science at Montana State University in the late seventies, Diane Ross found her eye increasingly drawn to the weathered chairs and benches that anchored the many front porches of the area's log cabins.

"At that time, there was still a lot of that old log furniture around—beds, chairs, and tables from the 1800s," she recalls. "They were usually in the bunkhouses and sometimes even outside, because people didn't value them. I couldn't afford to buy the furniture, so I decided I would make it myself."

Ross made her first piece of furniture, a chair of bent willow copied from a picture in a magazine, in 1979. She has since made a name for herself through her craftsmanship, her versatility, her masterful sense of proportion, and her sensitivity to the natural world from which her work springs.

Although Ross's work embraces several styles—cowboy, Adirondack, and bent willow—it is inspired by rustic ranch furniture born in the Rockies. "I like the idea of continuity," she

"Softwoods have idiosyncrasies, but cherry is very gentlemanly. It doesn't have bad habits, it doesn't splinter or chip. It just does what you ask it and looks good."

says, "that I'm honoring something that's been done before, but bringing my interpretation to it."

Ross's rustic style ranges from case pieces with applied pole laid in geometric patterns to graceful bent-willow chairs. She makes large pieces—bookshelf and bar installations—as well as freestanding furniture—chairs, tables, beds. And she also makes smaller pieces—coat hangers, wall racks, mirrors, small boxes, and lamps. She works in willow, birch, lodgepole, burl, and dogwood and employs a lot of chokecherry and cherry. "It's totally different from willow and there's a whole different way of working with it," she says. "Softwoods have idiosyncrasies, but cherry is very gentlemanly. It doesn't have bad habits, it doesn't splinter or chip. It just does what you ask it and looks good."

Ross works mostly on commission but does supply work to a few galleries around the country. She has studied Native American traditions in depth over the years and frequently employs designs from that culture in her mosaic twig work. Ross often allows the wood itself to determine its destiny. "I like

rustic furniture because I get to play with the wood. To me that's the challenge and the best part of it. I have a conversation with it: I ask, 'Do you think you can do this?' It feels good to design something and have it turn out like you envisioned."

Ross works out of her well-outfitted home shop just outside of Bozeman, but it's her long river walks and hillside antler-hunting rambles that provide her materials and ongoing inspiration. "The western landscape influences me so much. I like mountains, buttes, prairies, and high desert. It's big, it makes you think big, and it gives you room for possibility."

Her aspen comes from Vermont, but she gathers all the chokecherry herself and has developed a unique aesthetic in pairing it with cherry, as in a table with chokecherry legs and a cherry top. "They're from the same genus. I figured they would go well together and they really do. I sand down the chokecherry bark so it's really a dark, bronzy red and feels like leather. It's quite phenomenal. It flows together with the cherry yet is still a rustic piece."

Japan has come knocking on Ross's door recently; she's considered expanding her business, maybe taking on a few helpers. "But I don't want to run a business," she says simply. "I want to be a furniture maker."

*Brian Goff of Harker Designs chose this unusual high-back chair to anchor a quiet corner—the perfect place for reading on an inclement Wyoming night. The night table showcases the twig inlay work of Diane Cole Ross, who also made the bed.*
Photo © 2000 David Swift.

*"Spirits Untamed," a hand-carved juniper and mahogany bed by Montana artist Amber Jean, captured both the Best Western Spirit and People's Choice Awards at the 1999 Western Design Conference. Amber Jean studied art in Philadelphia and Germany before completing her fine-arts degree at Montana State University and choosing wood as her medium. "Whether it's the surface form or the interior grain, wood offers endless sculptural possibilities. When I see something within the wood, I take after it initially with a chainsaw and power tools to release the form. But it is the quiet hours of hand carving, the physical touch and communion, that I crave the most," says the artist.* Photo courtesy of the artist.

A table of red leather and brass tacks from *Buck Flynn Company* is perfect for a cluster of family pictures in a bedroom on a buffalo and cattle ranch, hinted at by the longhorn head above the fireplace. The fireplace screen was custom made by Peter Fillerup of *Wild West Designs*. A chandelier from *New West* floats between exposed log work; a painting by Bill Schenck hangs above a cabinet made by *Sweetwater Ranch*. Photo © 2000 David Fitzgerald & Associates.

# Places of Rejuvenation

### BATHROOMS

After a full day of branding—breathing dust, smelling singed hair, dodging kicks, and listening to the mamas bawl for their calves—some might argue that the most important space in the house is the bathroom and the only important amenity is hot water. Of course, they'd be right. Conversely, the most satisfying bath may well be a plunge into a cold creek on a hot day, and there's a certain primal appeal associated with making a trip to the outhouse under a clear, starry sky.

Most successful bathing spaces balance privacy with functionality while allowing nature in. This restorative feeling of the great outdoors can be achieved through glass in place of windows, through rock showers open to the out-of-doors, through walls of river stone that create a grotto-like effect—even through completely outdoor showers. Tiles invite the outside in through color, shape, and imagery; exposed log walls mimic the forests; cabinets of weathered wood speak to old buildings now disintegrating back into the ground; cast-bronze hardware comes in the shapes of items found under the sky, from leaves to twigs to arrowheads. Fine craftsmanship has extended into every nook and cranny of the house, including the peaceful, secluded bathroom space.

A whimsical mirror for a kids' bath or an angular driftwood coat rack for hanging bathrobes and cowboy hats can personalize the most intimate space in the house. Ideally, one would emerge feeling as relaxed as after a soak in a thermal spring, as rejuvenated as after a plunge in a glacier-fed alpine tarn—only here you won't have to pick pine needles from your soap.

*In an artist's studio an array of influences come together: stained glass, a horse-collar mirror, Mission-style lamps, protruding log ends, and brushes and canvas—the accoutrements of a painterly life.*
Photo © 2000 Chase Reynolds Ewald.

*The outdoors comes inside this master bath of glass, tile, and hand-peeled logs by Cody builder Nic Patrick, accented by a naked-cowgirl light fixture by Tony Alvis, cast-bronze hardware by Peter Fillerup, and classic horse-collar mirrors.* Photo © 2000 Elijah Cobb.

*L. D. Burke's offbeat sense of humor is well suited to a kids' bunkroom in the log barn of a working ranch. The one-of-a-kind mirror is embellished with guns and the saying "Straight shooters never miss a meal."* Photo © 2000 David Fitzgerald & Associates.

The goal with a shower made from local river rock and edgeless glass, says Van Bryan of Apogee Architects, was to bring nature in by creating a grotto-like space. Still, the room retains a sense of shelter. "Not everyone wants to feel like they're standing outside when they're taking a shower," he points out. Photo © 2000 Lynn Donaldson.

A door made from aged wood and distressed green-painted cabinets in a bathroom designed by Maggie Tandysh of Associates III speak to the timelessness of the region. Photo: David O. Marlow.

*The peaceful, secluded space that is the bathroom balances privacy with functionality while allowing nature in through rock showers open to the outdoors in an old stagecoach stop at the UXU Ranch.* Photo © 2000 Dewey Vanderhoff.

# At Work and At Play

## STUDIES AND PLAYROOMS

In the West, the great outdoors is both office and playroom. But even the homesteader in his one-room soddy needed a warm, dry place to figure his accounts. Today's work spaces and play spaces have evolved, of course. While some folks still work at the kitchen table, it's much more common to find a carefully crafted environment dedicated to these activities.

For one couple who combine two traditional western occupations—cattle ranching and oil—in a family business, working together comes naturally. When they travel, they travel together, and when they stay at home in Oklahoma, they can work face-to-face across a traditional partners' desk they designed themselves. Their office is a snug room lined with bookshelves and filled out with one-of-a-kind pieces of handcrafted furniture. A reading chair with Indian-style ledger paintings, a side table of twisted juniper, desk chairs with beadwork and bone all offer character, warmth, durability, and originality. The pieces, all commissioned from craftsmen they know, remind them that the joy of working is in the pursuit of quality.

Quality is the byword in a drop-front writing desk created for a busy mother in northern Wyoming. Meticulously made of juniper and driftwood, with multiple cubbyholes, bronze arrow drawer pulls, a leather writing surface, and even a secret compartment underneath, this piece provides the perfect place for sipping tea and writing letters while a snowstorm rages outside. When the front is closed, the raven image on its facade, carved by Blackfoot Indian Rod Skenandore, seems to announce its purpose while guarding its contents. The desk's designer, Jim Covert, patterned the piece after a ladies' writing desk by Arts & Crafts designer Harvey Ellis; it even has ebony pegs in the style of architect brothers Greene & Greene. The applied half-sticks and carving, however—which speak to the thick forests, rocky heights, and animal kingdom beyond the walls—make it pure West.

"In good light," says Covert, "that raven carving looks like it has a tiny bolt of lightning

*Antique woodcarvings from the homeowner's trips to India add an exotic touch to a suite of furniture that includes a desk and candlestick holder by Covert Workshops, and an office chair by John Gallis. Jamie Wyeth's pumpkins grin down on the scene.* Photo © 2000 Elijah Cobb.

*Lester Santos made this cherry and juniper desk, with an intricately carved pencil-drawer front and its own lighting.* Photo © Elijah Cobb.

running to its throat, as though he's just received a message or is getting ready to deliver one. The raven, of course, is the messenger [in Plains Indian lore.] It's perfect for a writing desk."

When it's time for play, humor and whimsy claim their place in terrain well marked by craftsman L. D. Burke. A family room tucked in the trees in Colorado sets its tone not so much in the comfortably upholstered couch, the fireplace, nor the Taos-drum end tables but with Burke's leather-wrapped card table. Centered in the tabletop are the words "When the going gets tough, the tough go fishing," and a fishing knife is imbedded in a panel in each corner.

Sometimes the details make all the difference, says Debbie Hindman of the Denver design firm Associates III. "Most people just want western touches. In those cases, fun pieces like that are perfect."

Combining an office and game room may not be traditional, but with today's increasing number of open floor plans and multipurpose family spaces, it's an idea that can work. A home in Wilson, Wyoming, does so effectively by setting the work space into the wall itself, with plenty of cabinets below for office supplies and open shelves above for an ever-growing Native American pottery collection. A large billiard table commands attention, as does its overhead lighting fixture with stained glass in bold primary colors set in a cast-bronze framework with mounted-Indian figures. A seating area combines a wood-slab table supported by multiple branches with chairs of woven willow and others whose backs feature a breastplate motif.

Designer Brian Goff of Harker Design admits that family togetherness in an office setting isn't for everyone, but, after all, knocking pool balls around can be an effective way to think through a problem.

*A bar by New Creation Cabinetry speaks to summertime pursuits with its realistic depiction of trout working their way upstream amid river rocks and coursing water.* Photo © Rob Wilke.

*Robin Stater of Sierra Design Studio designed this slab-and-stump desk, which she had locally made in the Sierra Mountains, for a compact home office.* Photo courtesy of the artist.

*A desk and built-in bookcase by Ron Shanor of Wildewood Furniture is of blue-stained pine, with fir and pine burl details. The drawers are of log slab, with burled poles and natural branches.* Photo © 2000 Elijah Cobb.

*Pop artist Bill Schenck started designing furniture when he couldn't find what he wanted. His office suite applies a Pueblo Deco aesthetic to traditional Molesworth forms, topping the desk and credenza with cheerful red leather.* Photo courtesy of the artist.

It's a long ride from a high-rise penthouse apartment in New York City to a log cabin in Wyoming. But that's just the trip, metaphorically speaking, that John Gallis's furniture has made.

When Gallis first visited a relative in Wyoming in 1994, this native New Yorker had been the chief cabinetmaker for the design center at Bloomingdale's department store for fifteen years — making entertainment centers, wall units, computer desks, and other necessities of urban life for Manhattanites. He and his wife had been thinking about moving to a safer, less-crowded, more-family-oriented place when they drove through Cody. "It was so big; the air smelled so fresh. My wife and I just looked at each other and said, 'Why couldn't we live here?' " Looking back, he admits, "We were so naive when we came here. You fall in love with the area and don't think about how to make a living. But the nice thing about a small town is if you're good, people hear about it."

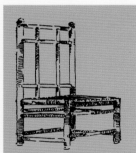

"A lot of this wood I slice myself; I'm the first person to see the grain. Each time it's like a treasure hunt. There's not a day that I get up and don't look forward to what I'm doing.

They were especially lucky to choose Cody, which has an active community of craftsmen and a major art museum. Cody also hosts the annual Western Design Conference. Gallis quickly developed a unique and distinctive "refined western" style that set him apart and earned him a spot at the 1996 conference. In 1997 his desk with three drawers captured the Exhibitors' Choice Award, in 1998 his roll-top desk won the People's Choice Award, and in 1999 he captured the title for Best Woodworking Craftsmanship. In addition to working with individual clients on commissions, his work is represented in four galleries around the West, guaranteeing a market for his functional art.

What sets Gallis apart are his choice of materials and his preference for curved lines over straight. His signature style employs walnut (although he also works in cherry and juniper), and positions the wood in such a way that the lighter-colored wood from the part of the tree closest to the bark forms a kind of outline for the piece, resulting in a halo effect. Thus, the footboard and headboard of a bed will feature the lighter wood along curved tops and on either side of "book-matched" vertical slats. The result is a design that is symmetrical and balanced but never rigid.

Gallis is humble about his achievements and passionate about his work. He often waxes eloquent on the merits of beautiful wood. "A lot of this wood I slice myself; I'm the first person to see the grain. Each time it's like a treasure hunt. There's not a day that I get up and don't look forward to what I'm doing.

Gallis continues, "People may say, 'How can this guy from New York know about western design?' But what is western design? It's organic; it's a feeling. And it can be whatever you want it to be."

*This phone table of juniper with walnut slabs by John Gallis is a bench and table rolled into one. The chair's crest rail shows the use of walnut sapwood that is Gallis's signature.* Photo © Elijah Cobb.

For a *Wild West Designs* chandelier over the pool table, designer Brian Goff of Harker Design chose bolder colors in the stained glass "for more emphasis, a little punch," he explains. The chairs with the breastplate motif are also from *Wild West Designs* and are paired with willow chairs and iron lighting by Christopher Thompson. Combining the work and play space makes sense for this homeowner, Goff says, though it may not be practical for every family. Photo © 2000 David Swift.

*A card table by master craftsman and humorist L.D. Burke adds whimsy to a western family room designed by Annette Stelmack of Associates III. She combined a comfortable sectional couch, Indian-drum end tables, and a coffee table of freestanding log sections by Mimi London.* Photo: David O. Marlow.

*Skip Odell of Larkspur, Colorado, designed this unusual mahogany game table with upholstered chairs to fit in a range of home styles, from western to more refined.* Photo courtesy of the artist.

This home office is a snug room lined with bookshelves and filled with one-of-a-kind pieces of handcrafted furniture—a reading chair of twisted juniper with ledger paintings and a side table of twisted juniper, both by Lester Santos, and desk chairs with bead-work and bone by Wild West Designs. The partner's desk was designed by the homeowner. Photo © 2000 David Fitzgerald & Associates.

Molesworth meets Art Deco in this mirror and cabinet of applied pole, brass tacks, and leather flanked by leather-upholstered Old Hickory-style barstools and reproductions of 1880s wrought-iron fixtures. Photo © 2000 Lynn Donaldson.

Amber Jean's Mountain Majesty gun cabinet features her remarkably detailed carving and painting. Photo courtesy of the artist.

Mike Elliott designed and built the bar-height table and chairs of aged Nevada cedar and sugar pine. Different colored hardwoods are used to create the inlaid pattern in the tabletop and chair backs. The horseshoe frame features triangular inlay, used horseshoes, and rope, with a hand-scalloped and burnt outer edge. Photo © 2000 Jeff Hinds.

# Creative Spaces

## GUEST QUARTERS AND OUTBUILDINGS

The West has always been a place to fulfill one's fantasies. Dreams become reality in the myriad creative applications for old buildings, traditional indoor/outdoor spaces, and single-purpose new spaces. Whether it's a room of one's own for the aspiring artist, a tented cabin for guest quarters, a sheep wagon converted to a writing den, a tepee for the kids' sleepovers, or an upscale outhouse, your reality is what you make it.

"Mainly, I needed a place to get away," admits an artist and mother of two. Though her work was interrupted by family life some years ago, she was able to pick up the paintbrush again when the children grew old enough for a full school day. A one-room cabin restored by Chris Taylor in Wapiti, Wyoming, became the perfect place for practicing art: simple and spare, with clerestory windows above the cabinetry and large vertical windows on two sides facing a dramatic valley rimmed by up-thrusting ridges. This studio has a functional side: along one wall are handmade cabinets above and a tiled countertop with flat shelving and vertical compartments below for drying and storing paintings. There is also a built-in desk and a sink for cleaning brushes. The rest of the space is unfurnished except for an easel—and one generously proportioned Molesworth-style chair facing the view. The floor is inset with an arrowhead motif that radiates from the base of the central log support post and serves as a perpetual reminder of the area's original artists.

When Breteche Creek Foundation planned their guest quarters, they felt it was essential to tread lightly on the land—this due to the preponderance of arrowheads and grizzly bear tracks found in a remote valley nearby. There, tented cabins take the place of permanent structures. A mix of camp equipment, homemade beds, and craftsman-made end tables make ideal guest cabins for summer use: primitive with sophisticated touches, comfortable while being outdoor-oriented. By day, guests can watch the patterns of leaves and branches shift across the canvas roofs. At night, they read by the light of Coleman lamps,

*A huge moose-antler chandelier dominates the scene in this homesteader's cabin, where a buffalo skull, antique guns, and wine bottles are paired with a walnut love seat by John Gallis and an applied-pole cabinet by New West, hand painted with Indian paintbrush, a wildflower found throughout the West.* Photo © 2000 Elijah Cobb.

*A one-room cabin restored by builder Chris Taylor became the perfect place for creating art. Simple and spare, with clerestory windows above the cabinetry and large vertical windows on two sides, the room faces a dramatic valley rimmed by up-thrusting ridges.* Photo © 2000 Elijah Cobb.

*Guest accommodations at Breteche Creek Ranch, a non-profit educational guest ranch in Wapiti, Wyoming, consist of ranch-made tented cabins. Furnishings include functional homemade bedsteads, end tables contributed by New West, a woodstove donated by a local outfitter, and the pattern of leaves on canvas.* Photo © 2000 Elijah Cobb.

listening to the wind, the creek tumbling past, the fire in the old camp stove, and the faint sound of belled horses in the nearby hills.

For the ultimate Old West–infused sleeping nest, nothing beats a sheep wagon. Not just remnants of the past, sheepwagons are still used today by sheepherders in remote parts of the Mountain West. Craftswoman Lynn Arambel has converted her indoor arena into a sheep wagon–renovation area. For her, wagons are both a link to the region's history and a romantic fantasy space.

They also lend themselves well to an entirely hand-crafted environment, and Arambel has added bay windows and oxidized-copper roofs as well as crafted the interiors. She prefers them simple, though, with just the sheepherder's stove and a handmade quilt on the bed. "I just love the space," she says. "I want to live in a sheepwagon on the side of a hill when I'm eighty."

A sense of history influenced Ham Bryan, owner of UXU Ranch in Wapiti, Wyoming, when building a deluxe cabin for his paying guests. On

a nearby ranch, he found a cabin for sale that had been a stagecoach stop for visitors on the way to Yellowstone. "Having that kind of history really interested me a lot. The fact of the matter," he concedes, "is that it's much more expensive to restore an old cabin than to build a new one—which I've since learned. But it's worth doing."

Bryan had the cabin deconstructed, moved, and restacked at the ranch. (He saved some of the old newspapers that had been used as insulation; they featured such items as notices of public hangings.) In the spring, local builder Chris Taylor did

*A century-old cabin offers a cozy retreat for guests at UXU Ranch in Wyoming, whose brand appears throughout on furniture created by New West. Ranch owner Hamilton Bryan had the logs taken apart and numbered. He waited until spring to have the cabin reconstructed on a site overlooking the North Fork of the Shoshone River. The goal, he said, was to "try to retain the feel and look of the cabin as built a hundred years ago but to make it comfortable for our guests."* Photo © 2000 Dewey Vanderhoff.

*Finding homestead cabins for restoring is becoming more difficult as their popularity increases. But for those who are fortunate enough to claim one for their own, nothing beats the coziness of a western soddy (so named for its sod roof) simply outfitted for retreat from the routine of everyday life.*
Photo © 2000 Chase Reynolds Ewald.

the reconstruction on a site overlooking the North Fork of the Shoshone River. The goal, he said, was to "try to retain the feel and look of the cabin as built a hundred years ago but to make it comfortable for our guests." (Thus, a 200-square-foot addition for bathrooms with indoor/outdoor showers.) Bryan worked with a local furniture maker to design everything from beds to sconces for the two-bedroom structure, all in the style of Cody furniture maker Thomas Molesworth. "We were trying to retain that Old West feel while bringing the outdoors in." Classic dude ranch furniture working with the textured log walls, rock showers from which one can hear the river rushing by, and fireplaces made of volcanic rocks collected on the ranch show that he succeeded.

Everyone has his own idea of what's western, her own vision of the perfect unique space. In today's West, says architect Van Bryan, "You see very different influences across the board. It happens because of the variety of clientele that comes here and the things they bring with them. People who originally moved here came from very diverse backgrounds, and it's still true today."

"Mostly what we're seeing are expressions that reflect the clients' lives, their passion for the West," notes designer Debbie Hindman. "They're saying, 'When I'm in the West, I want to feel like I'm in the West.'"

*Idaho artisan Tim Groth strives to be fresh and innovative in his designs. In the end, he says, "the beauty of the wood, through the curves, the twisting grains, and the exploding colors, speaks for itself."* Photo © Garth Dowling.

*Simple sturdy furniture, a little shade, and a burst of flowers are all that's needed in an outdoor space.* Photo © 2000 Chase Reynolds Ewald.

*A hand-forged gate by Colorado blacksmith Monty Powers suggests something unusual within.* Photo courtesy of the artist.

*Tepees have gained popularity throughout the West as guest rooms and camp-out spots. The interiors range from traditional—with grass floors and a fire ring—to fully outfitted with a suite of furniture. "It's a wonderful way to deal with seasonal guests in a very cost-effective manner, and also give visitors a real western experience in the bargain," says Mike Patrick of New West Furniture.* Photo © 2000 Chase Reynolds Ewald.

Lynn Arambel loves things with character born of age and adversity. "I do a lot of recycling," she says. "I love old things."

A recent project is a desk made from disassembled 150-year-old mesquite doors from Mexico. The door's panes became the drawer fronts, inset with old leather and framed in willow twigs. To add interest and authenticity, she reused the door's two-inch-long hand-carved pegs and left its bullet holes visible.

"I buy lots of tobacco-shed wood and train trestles—wood that is very old and dry. I just bought a batch of wood from old pickle vats. It's a lot more expensive than regular wood, but it has character." She makes beds out of old doors, porch posts, and finials, and fashions desks out of old gates. Arambel has maintained a thriving business restoring sheep wagons and refurbishing them as guest rooms or writer's dens.

A third-generation Wyoming rancher married to a sheep rancher, Arambel is a can-do kind of woman. She made her first piece of furniture at age eighteen, having learned craftsmanship at the knee of her grandfather. Winters, he lived with her family on the ranch outside Casper; summers, Arambel spent as much time as she could on the remote fishing lodge in British Columbia that he rebuilt one cabin at a time.

"That's how I learned to make furniture and restore cabins," she recalls. "The old furniture was great. There was a lot of lodgepole woven with rawhide, and there was a lot of that stuff made out of woven sticks, almost like wicker but woven. There were homemade tables, and a lot of it he made. There was no electricity; we used all hand tools. I'd go out and get logs and whittle them down and make a chair. I would go to my grandfather and say, 'Help me engineer this.' We'd sit down with a pencil and paper and figure it out. He was my mentor."

When she was seventeen she moved to Jackson, Wyoming, and took a job as a carpenter's helper. At age nineteen she spent a formative year living in a sheep wagon on the grounds of a little red schoolhouse where she worked as the janitor. In the 1970s, she became a cement chinker by trade, using authentic recipes containing sawdust and horsehair on historical forts and cabins such as those at Fort Casper. In 1989 Arambel started her furniture business.

"I had been working as a visual consultant, and my clients couldn't make up their mind about a piece of furniture. I said, 'Let's give it a face lift.' It was a Mission-style dresser that was in bad shape and we made it into a tall cabinet. We took the faces of the drawer fronts, which were spoon-carved and really cool, and old porch posts to become legs, and part of a picket fence and some willow twig work, and built another piece. Then their friends saw it and asked for something, and that's how it got going. I was just a single mom looking for work."

In the mid-1980s, Arambel was asked to rebuild a sheep wagon, launching yet another specialty. "I've done some where it just had the sheepherder's stove and a quilt on the bed, but mostly they're totally outfitted. I've done writer's dens, gypsy wagons, the cowboy look. The last two had copper tops on them, oxidized to look old. When we were kids, we were always playing in the sheep wagon. I always loved the space. I will live in a sheep wagon on the side of a hill when I'm eighty. I have such a passion for them."

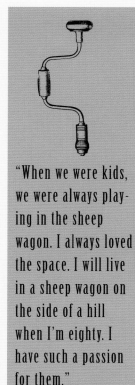

"When we were kids, we were always playing in the sheep wagon. I always loved the space. I will live in a sheep wagon on the side of a hill when I'm eighty. I have such a passion for them."

*Sheep wagons are still used today by sheepherders in remote parts of the Mountain West. For Wyoming native Lynn Arambel, who married into a Basque sheep-herding family, sheep wagons are romantic fantasy spaces that lend themselves well to an entirely hand-crafted environment.* Photo © Kay Lynn Reilly.

# Cowboy Chic Collection

*Moose and elk-antler love seat from Crystal Farm Antler Chandeliers.*
Photo courtesy of the artist.

*Love seat by Thome George.* Photo © Elijah Cobb.

*Dennis Judd fainting couch.* Photo courtesy of the artist.

*Spencer dining chairs in juniper with red leather by Marshall Dominick.* Photo courtesy of the artist.

*Bill Feeley's wildflower chandelier.* Photo courtesy of the artist.

*Eagle chandelier by Cash Metals.* Photo courtesy of the artist.

*Raku lamp with painted deer, applied antler, and pierced lampshade by David LaMure.* Photo courtesy of the artist.

*Bill Davis sculpted bronze elk lamp under Tiffany-style stained-glass lampshade.* Photo courtesy of the artist.

*A Northwest Native Designs roomscape combines a bucking horse leather-upholstered wing chair with Indian art, a Kokopelli lamp, and a northwestern totem paddle.* Photo courtesy of the artist.

*Rick & Rhonda Yocham's cowhide, leather & fringe daybed, now in the Buffalo Bill Historical Center.* Photo courtesy of Buffalo Bill Historical Center.

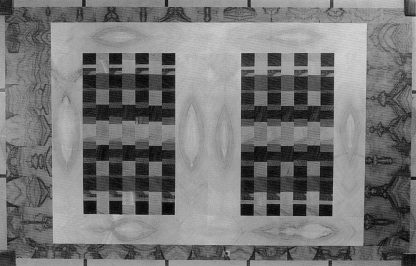

*Whimsy and humor are the bywords for Cody artist Wally Reber.* Photo courtesy of the artist.

*Mark Koon's inlaid mosaic hall table.* Photo courtesy of the artist.

Marshall Dominick's end table with a Russian olive slab top.
Photo courtesy of the artist.

Stage West's suede Nez Perce chest is accented with traditional
hair pipes, silver beads, antler pieces, and tin cones with horse.
hair. Photo courtesy of the artist.

# The Artisans

### FURNITURE WOODWORK

Amber Jean
1106 West Park #268
Livingston, MT 59047
406-222-8865
www.Amberjean.com
*Hand-carved, painted furniture.*

Antler Chandeliers & Lighting Co.
128 Miri Lane
Hamilton, MT 59840
888-226-8537
www.antlerchandeliers.com

Lynn Sedar Arambel
Ranch Willow Furniture
501 U.S. Highway 14
Sheridan, WY 82801
800-354-2830
*Hand-crafted willow furniture.*

*Anne Beard upholstered ottoman trio.* Photo © D. DeGabriele.

Anne Beard
Route 2, Box 2135
Heppner, OR 97836
541-676-9793
*Tailored clothing and ottomans.*

Bent Log Designs
PO Box 1494
Draper, UT 84020
800-Bentlog
www.bentlog.com
*Log furniture.*

Bergmeyer
229 North Hwy 33
Driggs, ID 83422
800-348-3356
*Manufacturer of traditional log furniture.*

Big Creek Willow
Dennis & MJ Judd
S15495 Canary Drive
Strum, WA 54770
715-695-3318
*Bent willow furniture.*

Big Sky Carvers
PO Box 507
Manhattan, MT 59741
800-735-7982
www.bigskycarvers.com

Black Dog Designs
Joseph Hegedus
1214 Van Buren
Missoula, MT 59802
406-721-6510
*Contemporary western furniture.*

James Boot
PO Box 755
St. Ignatius, MT 59865
406-745-3483

John Bryan Fine Art
198 Milliken Road
North Yarmouth, ME 04097
207-829-6447
www.bryanart.com
*Hand-carved mantelpieces.*

Michael Bryant's Juniper Furniture
Sunbird Gallery
916 NW Wall Street
Bend, OR 97701
541-389-9196
www.sunbirdart.com

Jack W. Burgess
PO Box 2361
Sun Valley, ID 83353
208-726-2566
jburgess@sunvalley.net
*Hand-carved tables & mantels.*

L. D. Burke, Cowboy Furniture
1105 Don Gaspar
Santa Fe, NM 87501
505-424-7322
*One-of-a-kind fun furniture.*

Chris Chapman
Chapman Designs
0075 Deer Trail Avenue
Carbondale, CO 81623
970-963-9580
*Leather-wrapped furniture.*

Martha Cieliesz
Just Tin Stuff
4721 Brookview Road
Rockford, IL 61107
815-397-4201
*Eclectic art furniture.*

Diane & Indy Corson
Lupine Arts
204 South Wallace
Bozeman, MT 59715
406-586-3480
lupineartsac@montana.net
*Kitchen furnishings, "cave-art" textiles.*

Jim Covert, Covert Workshops
2007 Public Street
Cody, WY 82414
307-527-5964
*Refined rustic furniture.*

Crystal Farm Antler Chandeliers
18 Antelope Road
Redstone, CO 81623
970-963-2350
cfarm@rof.net
*Antler chandeliers and furniture.*

Marshall Dominick
Sunlight Furniture
1019 Meadow Lane
Cody, WY 82414
307-587-9449
*Western furniture.*

Donnelly Designs Custom Furniture
463 Waterhill Lane
Stevensville, MT 59870
406-777-4366
www.donnellydesigns.com

Drawknife
516 North Hwy 33
Tetonia, ID 83452
800-320-0527
www.drawknife.com
*One-of-a-kind lodgepole billiard tables.*

Eastman Studios
Linda Sue Eastman
PO Box 1292
Winona, MN 55987
507-457-0918
*Tables, chests, and benches.*

Elkhorn Designs
PO Box 7663
165 North Center Street
Jackson, WY 83002
307-733-4655
cherokee@elkhorndesigns.com
*Antler furniture and lighting.*

Michael Elliott
Gardnerville, NV
702-265-9498
www.westernfurniture.net
*Inlaid frames and furniture.*

John Gallis
Norseman Designs West
814 36th Street
Cody, WY 82414
307-587-7777
*Refined western furniture and casework.*

Thome George
SweetTree Rustic
PO Box 1827
Tonasket, WA 98855
509-486-1573
*Willow furniture, unique lamps.*

Larry Green
PO Box 3916
Hailey, ID 83333
*Oversized cowboy and Indian chairs.*

Brad Greenwood
PO Box 164
Clio, CA 96106
530-836-0630
*Sophisticated rustic wood furniture.*

Grizzly Creek Log Builders
Jeff Murphy & Trent Stevens
PO Box 249
Parachute, CO 81635
800-349-6672
*Log and timber billiard tables.*

Tim Groth
P.M.B. 158
111 Broadway, Ste. 133
Boise, ID 83702
208-338-0331
*Western furniture.*

Hammerton's Mountain
Moose Collection
2149 South 3140 West
Salt Lake City UT 84119
801-973-8095
www.hammerton.com
*Iron furniture and accessories.*

Michael Hemry
930 Canyon Avenue
Cody, WY 82414
307-587-8135
*Arts & Crafts furniture.*

High Country Design
PO Box 5656
Frisco, CO 80443
970-468-1107
www.highcountrydesigns.com
*Refined rustic.*

High Mountain Design
Jon and Marie-Elena Kohler
HC 55, Box 331
Fishtail, MT 59028
406-328-6168
highmtnco@aol.com
*Tables with inset tiles.*

R.C. Hink
PO Box 1142
Bellevue, ID 83313
208-788-6020
*Weathered-wood furniture.*

Horseplay Furnishings
Mike and Carol Plummer
PO Box 3001
Mills, WY 83644
307-235-3316

JMJ Woodworking
Jack Moseley
70544 Buckhorn Road
Montrose, CO 81401
970-249-2891
*Wood lamps, carved shades.*

KCA Enterprises
Karry Hesla
6330 Dawn Drive
Belgrade, MT 59714
406-388-7759
www.westerntraditions.com
*Interesting painted screens.*

Don King
HC 67, Box 2079
Challis, ID 83226
208-838-2449
*Anthropomorphic chairs.*

King Ranch Saddle Shop
PO Box 1594
Kingsville, TX 78364-
1594
www.krsaddleshop.com
*Leather furniture and accessories.*

Mark Koons
1356 Maple Street
Wheatland, WY 82201
307-322-2127
mkoons@wyoming.com
*Japanese-influenced furniture.*

Mike Livingston
17 W. 5th Avenue
Hutchinson, KS 67504
316-662-2781
*Artisan wood furniture.*

Danial Steven MacPhail
1645 McKendree Church
Road
Kevil, KY 42053
270-488-2522
*Antler furniture and chandeliers.*

Rob Mazza
Willow Run Woodworking
2330 Amsterdam Road
Belgrade, MT 59714
406-388-6848
*Lodgepole and iron furniture.*

T. B. McCoy
439 Auburn Street
Grass Valley, CA 95945
530-477-9560
*Neo-Molesworth furniture.*

Anne McDaniel
PO Box 157
Costilla, NM 87524
505-586-0255
mcram@laplaza.org
*Rustic furniture.*

R. Dana Merrill Designs
PO Box 252
North Fork, ID 83466
208-865-2266
www.danamerrill.com
*Reclaimed wood furniture.*

*Twig-inlay buffet with fish by Anne McDaniel.* Photo courtesy of the artist.

Greg Mitchell
Legendary Furniture
1768 Woolsey Avenue
Fayetteville, AR 72703
501-444-3352
www.legendaryfurniture.com

Montana Wagons
Hilary Heminway and
Terry Baird
PO Box 1
McLeod, MT 59052
406-932-4350
*Sheep wagons & retreats.*

*T. B. McCoy's leather-upholstered chair.* Photo courtesy of the artist.

Montana Western Furniture
Russell and Rusty Viers
65 Billman Lane
Livingston, MT 59047
406-222-7564

Clifton Monteith
P.O. Box 165
Lake Ann, MI 49650
616-275-6560

John Mortensen
Mortensen Collection
PO Box 746
Wilson, WY 83014
307-733-1519
*Wood & cast-bronze furniture.*

New Creation Cabinetry
Matthew Crocker
21 Barnett Lane
Bozeman, MT 59715
406-522-9644

New West Furniture
J. Mike Patrick
2811 Big Horn Avenue
Cody, WY 82414
800-653-2391
*Western furniture and accessories.*

Northwest Native Designs
Ernie Apodaca
6404 130th Street SE
Snohomish, WA 98296
800-322-3599
*Custom leather couches and chairs.*

Skip Odell
Odell Woodworking
12447 Perry Park Road
Larkspur, CO 80118
303-681-3417
*Custom wood furniture.*

Old Hickory Furniture
403 South Noble Street
Shelbyville, IN 46176
800-232-2275
www.oldhickory.com

Pat Olson Furniture Art
812 Kimball Avenue, Unit C
Grand Junction, CO
81501
970-245-3055
Olson812@aol.com
*One-of-a-kind art furniture.*

*Doug Tedrow, Wood River Rustics, applied twig armoire.*
Photo courtesy of the artist.

John Omohundro
3765 South 19th
Bozeman, MT 59718
406-585-2699
johnyo2@yahoo.com
*Unique wood tables & chairs.*

Paisley Custom Wood
Products
Joe & Paige Paisley
PO Box 488
Meeteetse, WY 82433
307-868-2692
*Wood-inlaid furniture and
lamps.*

Peel Furniture Works
Dale R. Peel
565 West Main Street
Mt. Pleasant, UT 84647
435-462-2887
peelfurn@burgoyne.com
*Mormon pioneer furniture.*

Greg Race
Quandary Design, Inc.
408 West 3rd Street
Leadville, CO 80461
719-486-3498
www.quandarydesign.com
*Unique limited-edition
furniture.*

Ragged Mountain Antler
Chandeliers
PO Box 1164
Hamilton, MT 59840
406-961-2400
www.antlerchandelier.com

Wally Reber
1001 Aspen Drive
Cody, WY 82414
307-587-5819
*Whimsical western furniture.*

Red Bird Furniture
Rocky & Tawnya Wilson
PO Box 1313
Dubois, WY 82513
307-455-3153
*Custom lodgepole furniture.*

Rocking C & D Designs
Chuck & Deb Miller
6414 SW CR 0070
Corsicana, TX 75110
903-872-7860
*Hand-carved wood furniture.*

Rocky Mountain Granite &
Marble
Rob & Tammy Chriss
320 C Street
Cody, WY 82414
307-587-4162
*Natural stone installations.*

Rocky Mountain Log
Furniture
PO Box 3124
Idaho Springs, CO 80452
800-305-6030

Diane Cole Ross
Rustic Furniture
10 Cloninger
Bozeman, MT 59718
406-586-3746
*Refined rustic furniture.*

Round Valley Iron &
Woodworks
Vance and Joanne Paulson
PO Box 3744
Bozeman, MT 59772
406-582-0929
www.avicom.net/roundvalley
*Arts & Crafts western.*

Andy Sanchez
205 South Main Street
Belen, NM 87002
505-864-2003
*Southwestern juniper
furniture.*

Lester Santos
Arcadia Woodworks
2208 Public Street
Cody, WY 82414
888-966-3489
307-587-6543
www.arcadiawoodstudio.com
*Handcrafted, hand-carved
furniture.*

Bill Schenck &
Steve Alvorsen
268 Los Pinos Road
Santa Fe, NM 87505
505-424-6838
*Neo-western furniture.*

Ron & Jean Shanor
Wildewood Furniture
PO Box 1631
Cody, WY 82414
307-587-9558
www.wildewoodfurniture.com
*Wood furniture with burls.*

Ken Siggins
Triangle Z Ranch Furniture
PO Box 995
Cody, WY 82414
307-587-3901
siggins@wave.park.wy.us
*Classic ranch furniture.*

Silver Creek Antler
Company
PO Box 3463
Glenwood Springs, CO
81602
970-945-0507

Stage West
D. Rawlings & Sons Inc.
PO Box 3100
Cody, WY 82414
307-527-6620
SunBasin@juno.com
*19th-century-style trunks.*

Doug & Janice Tedrow
Wood River Rustics
PO Box 3446
Ketchum, ID 83340
208-726-1442
*Pine and willow furniture in
the rustic tradition.*

Tortuga Forge
R.C. Merrill
PO Box 1843
Gilbert, AZ 85233
888-867-8842
tortugaforge@juno.com
*Furniture with bronze accents.*

Reidar Wahl
1424 E. North Boyer Ave.
Sandpoint, ID 83864
208-255-2683
*Scandinavian western
furniture.*

Watagua Creek
232 NE Main Street
Franklin, NC 28734
800-443-1131
www.wataguacreek.com
*Western-furniture manufacturer.*

Willow Insights
Carla Jean Thistle
PO Box 87
Cazadero, CA 95421
707-632-5506
*Peeled willow furniture and
mirrors.*

Mike Wilson
Big Horn Antler and
Furniture Design
PO Box 306
Jackson, WY 83001
307-733-3491

Rick & Rhonda Yocham
Custom Leather Saddlery &
Cowboy Decor
Route 1 Box 536A
Bartlesville, OK 74006
918-335-2277
*Western furniture.*

METALWORK,
LIGHTING,
ACCESSORIES

Ace Billiard Co.
2465 Main Street
Sunset, UT 84015
888-300-POOL
www.acebilliard.com
*Custom lodgepole billiard tables.*

George Ainslie
Prairie Elk Forge
202 First Avenue East
PO Box 234
Lavina, MT 59046
406-636-2391
*Hand-forged metal items.*

Tony Alvis
Wilderness Iron Works
1275 West Main
Ventura, CA 93001
805-648-2113
*Light fixtures & fire screens.*

*Ken Siggins's Indians and
cavalry foosball table, detail.*
Photo courtesy of the artist.

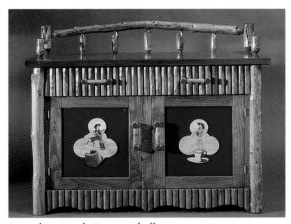

*Triangle Z Ranch Furniture buffet.* Photo courtesy of Triangle Z.

*Willowleaf mirror with native wildflowers and birds.* Photo courtesy of Willowleaf.

Jerry Wayne Bement
J. Dub's
641 Bumpy Lane
Ellensburg, WA 98926
800-622-9015
www.jdubs.com
*Custom ironwork.*

Robert Blanchet
PO Box 4
47 Mustang Drive
Dubois, WY 82513
307-455-2568
*Hand-painted parfleche art.*

Carpet Inspirations
Beth Whalen
400 South Emmett
Butte, MT 59701
406-782-4917
*Hand-carved carpets and rugs.*

Cash Metals
John & Kerry Cash
2803 Big Horn Avenue
Cody, WY 82414
307-587-2449
*Artisan metalwork.*

Cloudbird
P.O. Box 1827
Tonasket, WA 98855
509-486-1573
*Metal lamps with beadwork accents.*

Lynda Covert
Queen of the Plains
2007 Public Street
Cody, WY 82414
307-527-5964
*Hand-beaded leatherwork.*

Bill Davis
PO Box 50
Wapiti, WY 82450
307-527-7634
*Bronze-sculpted floor lamps.*

Featherstone
61535 South Hwy 97, Ste.
9-245
Bend, OR 97702
888-333-8556
*Hand-painted wall coverings.*

Bill Feeley Art 'N' Iron
PO Box 2245
Cody, WY 82414
307-587-5194
*Wrought-iron fire screens.*

Peter M. Fillerup
Wild West Designs
PO Box 286
Heber, UT 84032
435-654-4151
*Lighting fixtures and bronze work.*

Frontier Ironworks
391 Trabing Road
Buffalo, WY 82834
800-687-6952
www.frontierironworks.com
*Fire screens and other iron work.*

Glenn Gilmore
PO Box 961
Hamilton, MT 59840
406-961-1861
*Custom fire screens and tools.*

Inyan Kara Studios
K.T. Rainwater
PMB 414, 970 West
Broadway
Jackson, WY 83001
307-276-7722
*Carved & painted lamps.*

Judd's Inc.
3325 N. Val Vista
Mesa, AZ 85213
602-832-3683
*Handcrafted metal furniture.*

David LaMure Jr.
3307 E. 3200 North
Kimberly, ID 83341
208-736-0845
dlamure@rmci.net
*Raku vessels and lamps.*

La Unica Cosa
117 North Pueblo Road
PO Box 1644
Taos, NM 87571
800-748-1756
*Handspun wool pillows.*

M.C. Limited
PO Box 17696
Whitefish, MT 53217
800-236-5224
*Steer-hide rugs and pillows.*

MKR Design
1504 East North Avenue
Milwaukee, WI 53202
414-273-0463
www.homefurnishings.com
*Hand-tufted wool rugs.*

Mountain Moose Design
2149 South 3140 West
Salt Lake City, UT 84119
888-973-8095
www.mountainmoose.com
*Lighting fixtures.*

Penrose
Steve & Mary Lynn Blood
PO Box 295
Boston, NY 14025
716-941-0322
*Western lighting and accessories.*

Pony Trail Designs
Mike Flanagan
PO Box 57
450 East Second
Dayton, WY 82836
307-655-2350
*Sculpted furniture.*

Powers Forge North
Monty Powers
12555 WCR 2 1/2
Brighton, CO 80601
303-756-7248
www.bucknakedcowboys.com
*Tables and lighting fixtures.*

Red Arrow Metalcraft
Gerhard Pierson
PO Box 458
Powell, WY 82435
307-645-3155
*Torch-cut steel lamps and bookends.*

Rocky Mountain Hardware
PO Box 4108
Hailey, ID 83333
888-788-2013
www.rockymountainhardware.com
*Handcrafted bronze hardware.*

Santa Fe Door Source
Brian and Doris Fourchheimer
418 Cerillos Road, Suite 20
Santa Fe, NM 87501
505-995-9644
*Western Legacy line.*

Willowleaf Design
Leslie Northrup & Gregg Goodyear
PO Box 12833
Jackson, WY 83002
307-690-4493
*Rustic, hand-painted mirrors.*

## GALLERIES & RETAIL SOURCES

Anteks
8466 Melrose Avenue
Los Angeles, CA 90069
323-653-0810
*Western furnishings stores.*

Big Horn Gallery
1167 Sheridan Avenue
Cody, WY 82414
307-527-7587
*Fine art and furniture.*

Cabin Creek Home Furnishings
1402 - 17th Street
PO Box 734
Cody, WY 82414
307-587-9800

Cayuse
PO Box 1006
Jackson, WY 83001
307-739-1940
www.cayusewa.com
*Cowboy, Indian, & national park antiques.*

Djuna
Cherry Creek
221 Detroit Street
Denver, CO 80206
303-355-3500

The Elements
580 Main Street,
PO Box 771
Park City, UT 84060
435-649-4475
www.theelements.com

Fighting Bear Antiques
35 East Simpson
Jackson, WY 83001
307-733-2669
*Molesworth, Arts & Crafts antiques.*

Into the West Gallery
PO Box 880767
Steamboat Springs, CO 80488
800-351-8377

Marc Taggart & Co.
831 Canyon Avenue
Cody, WY 82414
307-587-9382
mtaggart@wtp.net
*Original Molesworth furniture.*

Martin-Harris Gallery
60 East Broadway
Jackson, WY 83001
800-366-7814
*Fine art & fine furniture.*

Old West Antiques
1215 Sheridan Avenue
Cody, WY 82414
307-587-9014

Timber Creek
1371 Sheridan Avenue
Cody, WY 82414
307-587-4246
*Furnishings & interior design.*

Topnotch
620 Sun Valley Road
Ketchum, ID 83340
208-726-7797
topnotch@micron.net
*Furnishings & interior design.*

### ARCHITECTS, BUILDERS, INTERIOR DESIGNERS

Mort Aker Architects
143 East Meadow Drive
Vail, CO 81657
970-476-5105

Apogee Architects
21 W. Babcock
Bozeman, MT 59715
406-585-5569
apogee@avicom.net

Associates III Interior Design
1516 Blake Street
Denver, CO 80202
303-534-4444

Big Timberworks Inc.
Box 368
Gallatin Gateway, MT 59730
406-763-4639
www.bigtimberworks.com
*Post-and-beam structures.*

Butterbrodt Design Associates
Rancho Santa Fe, CA 92067
858-792-5400

Chateau Cadeau
135 West Lake Boulevard
PO Box 170
Tahoe City, CA 96145
530-583-5101

Cottle Graybeal Yaw Architects
37347 U.S. Highway 6, Ste. 200
Avon, CO 81620
970-748-1516

Clair W. Danes
Bozeman, MT
406-586-9519

Dubbe-Moulder Architects
PO Box 9227
1160 Alpine Lane
Jackson, WY 83002
307-733-9551
www.dubbe-moulder.com

Rudi Fisher Architects
PO Box 641
Vail, CO 81658
970-949-5624

Jonathan Foote
126 East Callender
Livingston, MT 59047
406-222-6866

Gallinger Trauner Design
3785 S. Lake Creek Drive
Wilson, WY 83014
307-733-0902

Green's Timberworks Custom Builders
406-585-2494
www.timberframemontana.com

Harker Design
3465 North Pines Way, Ste. 101
Wilson, WY 83014
800-473-4369
www.harkerdesign.com

Hilary Heminway
140 Briar Patch Road
Stonington, CT 06378
860-535-3110

Home Outfitters
Jennifer Williams
415 West Lewis
Livingston, MT 59047
406-222-8525

Will Hooper, Designer
154 West 13th Street
New York, NY 10011
212-255-4289

Jackson Moore Ltd.
130 East Broadway
PO Box 12229
Jackson, WY 83002-2229
307-734-2425
www.jacksonmoore.com

Kent Interiors
533 Mendenhall
Bozeman, MT 59715
406-587-8900

LaChance Builders
Swift Creek Ranch
395 Del Rey Road
Whitefish, MT 59937
406-862-5597
www.lachancebuilders.com

Kirk Michels, Architect
409 East Callender
Livingston, MT 59047
406-222-8611

Montana Log Homes
PO Box 771865
Steamboat Springs, CO 80477
970-879-3031

Ellis Nunn & Associates Architects
PO Box 7778
Jackson Hole, WY 83002
307-733-1779

Rob Rogers
Rogers Marvel Architects
145 Hudson, 3rd Fl.
New York, NY 10013
212-941-6718

Sierra Design Studio
Robin Stater
PO Box 1280
Mammoth Lakes, CA 93546
760-934-4122

Sun Valley Log Homes
PO Box 452, Highway 75
Bellevue, ID 83313
208-788-4715

Chris Taylor, Woodsmythe
120 RD 6FU
Wapiti, WY 82450
307-587-3225

Yellowstone Traditions
Harry Howard & Dennis Derham
Box 1933
Bozeman, MT 59771
406-587-0968

### CONFERENCES & AUCTIONS

Old West Show & Auction
PO Box 655
Cody, WY 82414
307-587-9014
oldwest@cody.wtp.net
*Cowboy collectibles and antiques show, held annually in June.*

Western Design Conference
1108 14th Street, #105
Cody, WY 82414
888-685-0574
www.westd.org
*Held annually in late September.*

www.theamericanwest.com
*Old-west merchandise and auction site.*